DIGITAL COMPUTER LABORATORY

GRADUATE COLLEGE

UNIVERSITY OF ILLINOIS

ILLIAC PROGRAMMING

A Guide to the Preparation of Problems

for Solution by

the University of Illinois Digital Computer

URBANA, ILLINOIS
March 1, 1954

PREFACE

The Digital Computer Laboratory of the University of
Illinois has a three-fold program which is concerned with research in the field of digital computers, with maintenance for
University use of a high-speed digital computer, and with teaching
of design and use of digital computers. The preparation of programs for the Illiac is the responsibility of the person who wishes
his problem solved. But since each prospective user cannot always
attend the courses on programming offered by the University, it
has seemed desirable to help make it possible for him to learn
the elements of Illiac use by himself.

The result has been this book, which makes use of a
year's experience in operating the Illiac for University research
and several years experience in the teaching of programming.
Many of the chapters were used in preliminary form as supplementary
material in Mathematics 385, the basic course on programming.

The book, like most of the work of the Digital Computer
Laboratory, is the result of a group effort by many different people.
The chapters were written by S. Gill, R. E. Meagher, D. E. Muller,
J. P. Nash, J. E. Robertson, T. Shapin and D. J. Wheeler. Other
members of the laboratory staff read the material and offered
valuable criticism. The typewritten copy was prepared by
Natalie R. House and Caroline M. Brown; the drawings were made by
George Ehrlich.

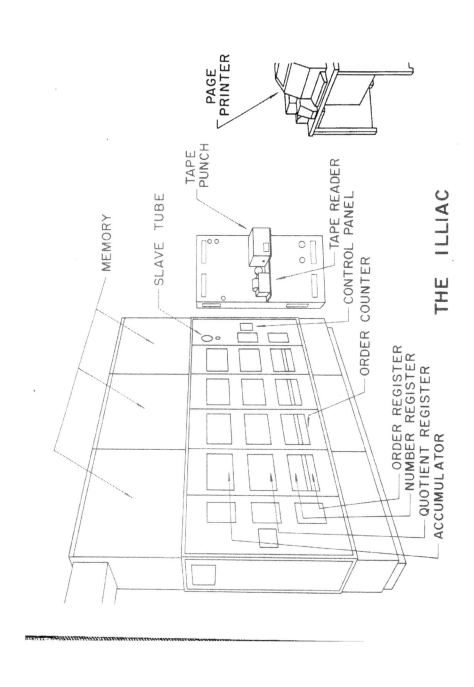

MEMORY

SLAVE TUBE

TAPE PUNCH

PAGE PRINTER

TAPE READER

CONTROL PANEL

ORDER COUNTER

ORDER REGISTER

NUMBER REGISTER

QUOTIENT REGISTER

ACCUMULATOR

THE ILLIAC

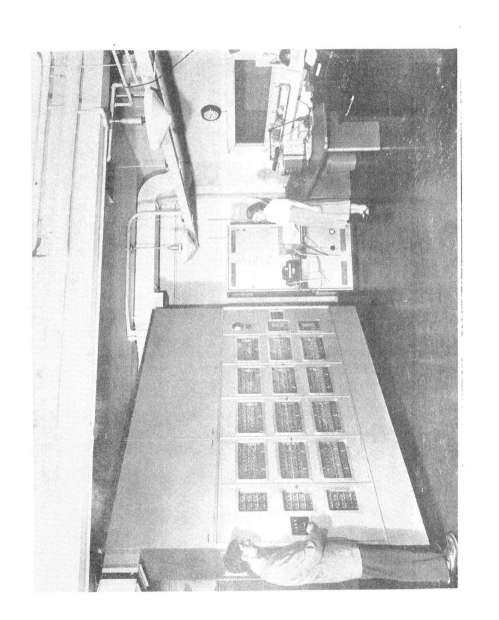

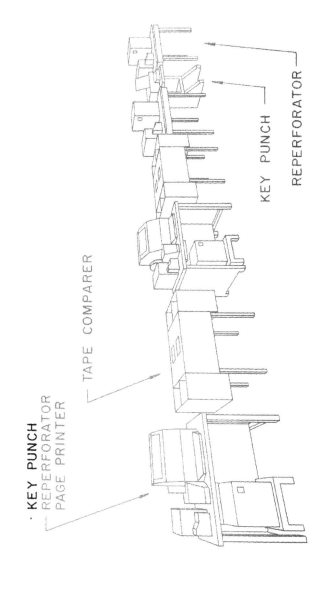

KEY PUNCH
REPERFORATOR
PAGE PRINTER

TAPE COMPARER

KEY PUNCH

REPERFORATOR

TAPE PREPARATION EQUIPMENT

CONTENTS

CHAPTER 1

INTRODUCTION

In 1948 the University of Illinois began to look into the
possibility of acquiring an automatic digital computer. When attempts
to buy one or to have one built failed, the University decided to
build one of its own, and the Digital Computer Laboratory was organized
in February 1949. Shortly thereafter an agreement was made to build
a second computer for the Army to be used at the Aberdeen Proving
Ground.

It was decided to build the two machines following the design of a computer then being designed and built at the Institute for
Advanced Study. While many modifications were later made, both
machines built by the University owe much to the early designs obtained from Princeton.

The two machines were built more or less together so that
advantage could be taken of the savings obtainable by paralleling
the design and construction work, but work on the Army machine, called
the ORDVAC, was emphasized, and it was finished first. It passed its
acceptance tests in February 1952 at Aberdeen and it has been in use
there since that time.

Work on the University computer (later named the Illiac) was
completed in September 1952 and the computer was first made available
for University use when classes began on Monday, September 22, 1952.

The Illiac is an automatic electronic digital computer.

It is digital because it handles numbers as sets of digits which have discrete values, rather than as scale readings or measurements, which are continuously variable. Apparatus for handling digits is more complicated than that for handling continuous quantities, but it is capable of giving unlimited accuracy by using suitable numbers of digits.

The Illiac is electronic. In the last ten years electronic circuits for storing, transmitting, adding, subtracting, multiplying and dividing numbers in digital form at extremely high speeds have been devised. The actual addition of two numbers in the Illiac takes only about 75 microseconds.

Such speed is useless unless the machine can be made to go ahead on its own with many thousands of operations, without human intervention. The Illiac is therefore automatic, in the sense that it can be given orders telling it how to proceed, and will then act on these orders automatically.

In common with many other computers of a similar type, the Illiac contains the following five essential features:

(1) An arithmetic unit.

(2) A memory or store.

(3) Devices for the input and output of
     information (e.g. numbers) to and
     from the machine.

(4) Means for the transfer of information
     between the various parts of the machine.

1-2

(5)   Means for the automatic control cf
        the whole machine.

The arithmetic unit carries out the individual arithmetical operations
that make up every computation; it can be thought of as the electronic
equivalent of a desk calculating machine. It is described in detail
in Chapter 2.

        The memory is needed because, in any lengthy calculation,
numbers produced at early stages of the calculation are frequently
required to be used at later stages; they must therefore be recorded
or "remembered". The memory is capable of recording 1024 numbers.
These can be recorded (i.e. transferred to the memory from the arithmetic unit) individually, as directed by the computer's control device, and recalled again individually in a similar way. The memory
may be thought of as 1024 little boxes or locations, each accomodating
one number, and labelled with the numbers 0 through 1023. The label
of a location is called its address. A number in the memory is
identified by the address of the location containing it.

        Information enters and leaves the Illiac coded in the
form of a pattern of holes in punched paper tape; there is a tape
reader for input, and an automatic punch for output. There is also
a teletypewriter which can be used to provide output from the machine
directly in printed form. Several machines are available for preparing punched tape, copying it, comparing it, and producing printed
versions of the information on it.

1-3

The problem of controlling the whole computer has been solved by stipulating that every individual operation that occurs within the machine must be one of a certain set of specified permissible operations, and that no two such operations can occur simultaneously. Thus the design problem was reduced to that of engineering the various permissible operations and arranging for them to be executed in any desired sequence. It is up to the user of the Illiac to specify the sequence of operations or program, which the Illiac must execute to carry out his calculation.

Each permissible operation can be specified in a concise coded form called an order. The correspondence between the set of permissible operations and the set of orders which specify them is called the order code of the Illiac. It is given in detail in Chapter 3. A coded problem is called a program or routine.

The machine's control unit has the task of accepting orders one by one, and of causing the machine to carry out the operations specified according to the order code. If each order were taken by the control unit directly from a punched tape, then to make full use of the speed of the rest of the machine the tape would have to pass through the tape reader at about 200 miles per hour. Instead, the orders are recorded in the memory along with the numbers, so that the control unit merely has to take its orders from the memory, which it can do electronically at high speed. This is made possible by coding each order to look like a number. To be more precise, orders are

1-4

stored in pairs, one pair to a memory location.   The information
contained in one memory location is often called a word, meaning
either a number or an order pair. Of course, the more orders there
are in the memory, the less room there is for numbers. Both orders
and numbers are fed into the machine initially on punched tape.

Normally orders are obeyed by the control unit in the sequence in which they are stored in the memory, e. g.:

> Left-hand order in location 6,
> Right-hand order in location 6,
> Left-hand order in location 7,
> Right-hand order in location 7,
> Left-hand order in location 8, etc.

Sometimes, however, this sequence is broken and the control unit
starts over at some new position in the memory; this is called a
transfer of control.   There are special orders which cause this.
There is also special provision for making a transfer of control depend
on the value of some number obtained by the machine during the calculation. Thus the machine can be made to "choose" one of two or more
alternative courses of action according to the way things happen to
work out.

If control is transferred a few locations back in the memory,
the machine will repeat the operations specified by the intervening
orders. It is possible to cause this repetition to occur any number
of times, leading to a cyclic behavior of the machine. Practically

every calculation which the machine performs contains several such cycles, often one inside another. In this way it often happens that the same order gets carried out many thousand of times, so that a few orders suffice to keep the machine busy for several minutes. If each order in the memory were to be carried out once only, the Illiac would get through them all in a quarter of a second (even if the memory contained nothing but orders). In practice, calculations vary in duration from a minute to a few hours.

The occurrence of cycles is one of the things that complicates the programming of a calculation. Another is the fact that, since orders are stored in the memory in the same form as numbers, they can be operated on and altered during the course of a calculation (at the behest of other orders) just as if they were numbers. All this makes possible some most interesting calculations; it can also make programming difficult.

Fortunately a coder can often, as described in Chapter 4 make use of bits of programming done by other people. Thus a typical program consists of a number of groups of orders, some written by the coder, others already available. The latter will be available in punched tape form, and can be copied mechanically onto the program tape along with the new orders. Tape preparation is described in Chapter 9.

When the whole tape for a particular program has been prepared it can be placed in the tape reader of the Illiac. The Illiac reads the tape, forms the orders and numbers punched on it and stores them

in the memory. When the program is in the memory, the machine begins
to execute the orders, continuing until it comes to some particular
order which causes it to stop. If the programming is correct, this
is the end of the calculation. If there is a mistake in the programming
various things may happen; remedies are discussed in Chapter 8.

Somewhere in the program will be some orders which cause
the machine to punch some output tape. This carries the results of the
calculation. The program may also contain orders causing the machine
to read more input tape, carrying data for the calculation.

The reading of most of the program tape is accomplished by
the Illiac executing a particular set of orders called the Decimal
Order Input (See Chapter 5) which is always punched at the beginning
of every program tape and hence read into the machine before the rest
of the tape. The Decimal Order Input not only assembles the program
inside the machine; it also makes certain modifications and conver-
sions, so that the way in which orders are represented when punched
is somewhat different from their final form in the memory. The
object is to make programming easier. It is important to remember that
the written form of an order and the form which it assumes in the
memory are not the same thing. The relationship between the two is
determined by the Decimal Order Input.

Remaining chapters of this manual are devoted to: The
arrangement of calculations so that all the numbers encountered
are the right size (Chapter 6); ways of programming certain types of

simple tasks (Chapter 7); how to estimate the duration of a calculation (Chapter 10); an example of a typical program (Chapter 11); and how the program library is organized (Chapter 13). Finally, concise descriptions of the principal contents of this collection are given.

CHAPTER 2

THE ARITHMETIC OF THE ILLIAC

The construction of a computer involves a compromise between engineering economies on the one hand and ease and flexibility of use on the other. As a result, the details of the operations of arithmetic are often dictated by engineering design considerations. The following paragraphs describe the peculiarities of the representation of numbers and of the operations of arithmetic in the Illiac.

2.1   REPRESENTATION OF NUMBERS.   The simplest device for storage of numerical information is an electronic element having two stable states in which one state is called "zero" and the other state "one".   One such element is capable of holding one binary digit. In the Illiac registers composed of forty such elements are provided for representation of forty binary digit numbers. The Illiac is described as a binary parallel digital computer having a precision of forty binary digits -- roughly equivalent to twelve decimal digits.

The Illiac is a fixed-point computer; the locations of the fixed binary point between the first and second digits is indicated in Figure 2.1.

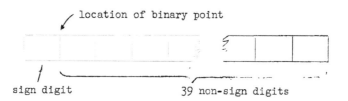

location of binary point

sign digit

39 non-sign digits

Figure 2.1

The Forty Digits of a Word

The leftmost digit of a number is the sign digit. If the sign digit is zero, the number is positive or zero; if the sign digit is one, the number is negative. For example, + 7/8 is represented in the Illiac as

$$0.11100 \ldots 00 = + 1/2 + 1/4 + 1/8 = +7/8$$

Negative Numbers. Negative numbers are represented in the Illiac as complements with respect to 2. The process of complementation is carried out by forming the digitwise complement (replacing ones by zeros and zeros by ones) and then adding a unit in the least significant (thirty-ninth) non-sign digit. As an example, - 7/8 is formed from + 7/8 by complementation as follows:

0.11100	... 00	+ 7/8
1.00011	... 11	ones replaced by zeros and zeros by ones
+ 0.00000	... 01	addition of 2^{-39}
1.00100	... 00	machine representation of - 7/8

It is sometimes essential to distinguish between the

machine representation of a number and its arithmetic value. Suppose
we have a number whose arithmetic value is x and whose machine representation has the sign digit x_0 and non-sign digits $x_i (i = 1,2,...,39)$.
If x is positive; i.e., if $x_0 = 0$, then

$$x = \sum_{i=1}^{39} 2^{-i} x_i. \tag{2.1}$$

If x is negative $(x_0 = 1)$, then the relationship is

$$x = -1 + \sum_{i=1}^{39} 2^{-i} x_i. \tag{2.2}$$

Equations 2.1 and 2.2 may be combined in the one equation

$$x = -x_0 + \sum_{i=1}^{39} 2^{-i} x_i. \tag{2.3}$$

If equations 2.1 through 2.3 are to hold, x must be restricted to
the range $-1 \leq x < 1$. The programmer must keep in mind that the
Illiac arithmetic unit is designed for numbers in the range $-1 \leq x < 1$.
When an operation is performed which yields a number outside this
range, an unwanted number within the range results. This effect is
called overflow and, although certain operations are unaffected by
overflow, computational errors usually result.

2.2   FUNDAMENTAL OPERATIONS OF THE ILLIAC ARITHMETIC UNIT.
The following five operations are fundamental in the arithmetic unit

of the Illiac:

1. complementation,

2. addition,

3. left shift, or multiplication by two,

4. right shift, or division by two,

5. clearing to zero.

Complementation is executed in the Illiac in the manner described in the previous section by a circuit called a complement gate. The complement gate is actuated by a signal from the control and is capable of supplying either the number unchanged, or its digitwise complement. Addition is carried out by the adder, which is capable of forming the sum of two 40 binary digit addends.

A left shift is a displacement of the binary digits one digital position to the left and corresponds to a multiplication by two. There will be an overflow if the number to be shifted is + 1/2 or if it has an absolute value greater than one-half. The right shift is a displacement of the binary digits one digital position to the right and corresponds to a division by two. For example,

0.0111	shifted left is 0.1110;	$7/16 \times 2 = 7/8$
0.1110	shifted right is 0.0111;	$7/8 \div 2 = 7/16$
1.0010	shifted right is 1.1001;	$-7/8 \div 2 = -7/16$
1.0100	shifted left is 0.1000;	$-3/4 \times 2 = 1/2$ because of overflow.

It should be noted that the sign digit is propagated when the right shift is executed. The Illiac arithmetic unit has two shifting registers, each capable of executing both left and right shifts.

Clearing to zero involves setting all digits of a number to zero; the corresponding arithmetic value is zero.

2.3   THE ILLIAC ARITHMETIC UNIT.   The structure of the Illiac arithmetic unit is shown in Figure 2.2.   The arithmetic unit is composed of two shifting registers, the accumulator A and the quotient register Q, and one non-shifting register, the number register R^3. Also required are the complement gate and the adder. The A and Q registers are the only registers to which the programmer has direct access; the number register R^3 is used to hold temporarily the numbers brought from the memory for arithmetic operations. It is essential that the programmer be familiar with the roles played by the A and Q registers in the operations of arithmetic; many programming errors arise from placing operands in or removing results from the wrong register. The functions of the registers during the operations of arithmetic are described in the sections which follow.

2.4   ADDITIONS (Order Type L).   Before an addition instruction begins, the augend lies in the accumulator register A. During execution of the addition instruction, the addend is transferred from a specified memory location to the number register R^3. The digits of R^3 are then sensed through the complement gate unchanged, so that the addend forms one of the inputs to the adder. The augend in A is the second adder input. The adder forms the sum which is

2-5

transferred to the accumulator A, replacing the augend. The quotient
register Q is undisturbed by the addition instruction.

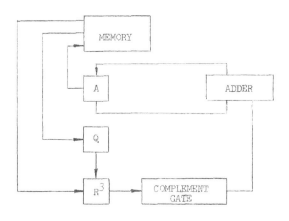

Figure 2.2

The Illiac Arithmetic Unit

Two variants of addition are "hold add" and "clear
add". The "hold add" instruction leaves the augend in A undisturbed until the sum is formed by the adder. The "clear add"
instruction clears A to zero initially, thus setting the augend
to zero. The "clear add" instruction is thus a transfer order
which moves a number from a specified memory location to the accumulator A.

2.5 SUBTRACTIONS (Order Type L). Subtraction in
the Illiac arithmetic unit is performed by adding the complement

2-6

of the subtrahend to the minuend. Before the subtract instruction

begins, the minuend lies in the accumulator A, and is used as one

of the two adder inputs. The subtrahend is brought from a specified

memory location to R^3; its complement is formed by the complement

gate and is used as the second adder input. The adder thus forms

the difference by forming the sum of the minuend and the complement

of the subtrahend. The adder output is then transferred to the

accumulator A, replacing the minuend.

Either the "hold subtract" instruction or the "clear

subtract" instruction can be used by the programmer. For the former

instruction, the result of a previous operation is left in the accumu-

lator A as minuend; for the "clear subtract", the minuend in A is

set to zero, so that A contains the negative of the number in a

specified memory location when the operation has ended.

2.6   ABSOLUTE VALUE ADDITION AND SUBTRACTION (Order Type L).

It is possible to form the absolute value of the addend (or sub-

trahend) after it has been transferred from a specified memory loca-

tion to R^3 and before it is added to the augend (or subtracted from

the minuend) in the accumulator. Ordinarily the setting of the com-

plement gate depends upon whether the instruction is an addition or

a subtraction; for forming the absolute value of the number in R^3,

it is necessary to sense the sign digit of R^3 as well. For example,

if the addition of the absolute value of a negative addend is re-

quired, the sign digit of the addend in R^3 is sensed indicating that

a complementation is necessary. The add instruction ordinarily does not require complementation; the net effect of the sensing of the add instruction and the R^3 sign digit is that the complement gate is set to form the complement of the addend.

    2.7   <u>INCREMENT ADD ORDERS</u> (Order Type F). It was noted in section 2.1 that the operation of complementation is performed by first forming the digitwise complement of the number held in R^3 and by then adding a unit in the least significant digital position of the adder. For the ordinary addition and subtraction orders (order type L), the least significant digit insertion occurs only when the complement gate is set to form the digitwise complement. In the Illiac, special increment add orders (type F) are provided. For these orders, the relationship between the setting of the complement gate and the insertion of the least significant digit is reversed. Thus, the "clear increment add" instruction sets the augend initially in A to zero and adds the addend from R^3 to 2^{-39} and places the result in A. Conversely, the "clear increment subtract" instruction sets the minuend in A to zero, replaces ones of the subtrahend by zeros and replaces zeros of the subtrahend by ones, and transfers the digitwise complement of the subtrahend thus formed from the adder to A. Detailed descriptions of further orders of this type are given on page 3-28.

    2.8   <u>ADD FROM Q</u> (Order Type S) <u>AND INCREMENT ADD FROM Q</u> (Order Type K) <u>INSTRUCTIONS.</u> For the add from Q and increment add from Q instructions, the addend or subtrahend is transferred to the number register R^3 from the Q register, rather than from a

specified memory location. Otherwise, the K and S order types
are the same as the corresponding F and L order types described in
sections 2.4 through 2.7.

2.9   THE SHIFT ORDERS (Order Types 0, 1).   Since the
right and left shift operations are fundamental in the Illiac
arithmetic unit, specific shift instructions are provided for the
programmer. All digits in both A and Q, except the sign digit q_o
of Q, are shifted. A left shift (order type 0) of one digital
position replaces

$$a_0, \; a_1, \; a_2, \; \cdots, \; a_{37}, \; a_{38}, \; a_{39} \text{ in A}$$

and

$$q_0, \; q_1, \; q_2, \; \cdots, \; q_{37}, \; q_{38}, \; q_{39} \text{ in Q}$$

by

$$a_1, \; a_2, \; a_3, \; \cdots, \; a_{38}, \; a_{39}, \; q_1 \text{ in A}$$

and

$$q_0, \; q_2, \; q_3, \; \cdots, \; q_{38}, \; q_{39}, \; 0 \text{ in Q.}$$

The right shift (order type 1) of one digital position replaces

$$a_0, \; a_1, \; a_2, \; \cdots, \; a_{37}, \; a_{38}, \; a_{39} \text{ in A}$$

and

2-9

$$q_0, \ q_1, \ q_2, \ \cdots , \ q_{37}, \ q_{38}, \ q_{39} \ \text{in Q}$$

by

$$a_0, \ a_0, \ a_1, \ \cdots , \ a_{36}, \ a_{37}, \ a_{38} \ \text{in A}$$

and

$$q_0, \ a_{39}, \ q_1, \ \cdots , \ q_{36}, \ q_{37}, \ q_{38} \ \text{in Q}.$$

From the behavior of the left and right shift we see that we may consider the shifting to take place in a single regis-ter AQ of 79 digits consisting of A followed by Q with q_0 deleted.

Thus the left shift replaces

$$a_0, \ a_1, \ a_2, \ \cdots , \ a_{37}, \ a_{38}, \ a_{39}; \ q_1, \ q_2, \ \cdots , \ q_{37}, \ q_{38}, \ q_{39}$$

by

$$a_1, \ a_2, \ a_3, \ \cdots , \ a_{38}, \ a_{39}, \ q_1; \ q_2, \ q_3, \ \cdots, \ q_{38}, \ q_{39}, \ 0$$

While the right shift replaces

$$a_0, \ a_1, \ a_2, \ \cdots, \ a_{37}, \ a_{38}, \ a_{39}; \ q_1, \ q_2, \ \cdots, \ q_{37}, \ q_{38}, q_{39}$$

by

$$a_0, \ a_0, \ a_1, \ \cdots, \ a_{36}, \ a_{37}, \ a_{38}; \ a_{39}, \ q_1, \cdots, q_{36}, \ q_{37}, \ q_{38}.$$

The number n of shifts can be specified in the address digits of the shift order by the programmer. A left shift of n digital positions replaces AQ by 2^n AQ. Similarly, a right shift of n digital positions replaces AQ by 2^{-n} AQ; n lies in the range $1 \leq n \leq 63$.

2.10 <u>MULTIPLICATION</u> (Order Type 7). Initially, the multiplier lies in the quotient register Q. At the beginning of the multiplication instruction, the multiplicand is transferred from a location specified by the address of the multiply order into the number register R^3, where it remains throughout the multiplication. The multiplication then consists of a sequence of additions and shifts. More precisely, a multiplier digit in q_{39} is sensed. There are two cases. (a) If $q_{39} = 1$, the multiplicand is added to the partial product in A. A right shift in AQ follows which halves the number in A and moves a new multiplier digit into q_{39} as well as transferrering a product digit from a_{39} to q_1. (b) If $q_{39} = 0$, only the right shift occurs, which transfers a_{39} to q_1 and transfers the next most significant digit of the multiplier into q_{39}. After thirty-nine right shifts have occurred, the sign digit of the multiplier is sensed. If the multiplier is positive, the multiplication is complete, with a double precision product (sign digit and seventy-eight non-sign digits) in AQ. For a negative multiplier x, the process of thirty-nine shifts and conditional additions constitutes a multiplication of the multiplicand y by $1 + x$ (Equation 2.3) to form a product $y(1 + x) = y + xy$. In this case the Illiac automatically subtracts the multiplicand y to produce the correct product xy.

A number of variations of the basic multiplication procedure described in the previous paragraph are possible. The initial contents of A may be either 0, 1/2, or some quantity previously calculated. If we designate the initial contents of A by a, the final double precision product in AQ is $xy + 2^{-39}$ a, where x and y are multiplier and multiplicand, respectively. For a = 0, the instruction specified is "clear multiply" and the result in AQ is the exact 78 digit signed product xy. For a = 1/2, the instruction specified is "roundoff multiply" and the result in A is a rounded 39 digit signed product. If a is arbitrary, the instruction specified is "hold multiply", and the result in AQ is $xy + 2^{-39}$ a; the quantity a is thus added to the least significant part of the product in Q. In all multiplication instructions the sign digit q_0 of the quotient register is set to zero.

For each of the three types of multiplication instructions described in the previous paragraphs, four additional variations can be specified by the programmer. Either N(n), -N(n), $|N(N)|$, or - $|N(n)|$ can be used as the multiplicand, where N(n) is the number transferred from memory location n to the number register R^3.

2.11   DIVISION (Order Type 6). Initially, the double precision dividend lies in AQ. The divisor is transferred at the beginning of the division instruction from a memory location specified by the address of the divide order to the number register

R^3. For positive divisor and dividend, the process is analogous to elementary long division. The divisor is subtracted from a partial remainder in A and the sign of the difference (in the adder) is sensed. If the difference is negative, 0 is inserted in q_{39} as quotient digit and AQ is doubled to form a new partial remainder. If the difference is positive, 1 is inserted in q_{39} as quotient digit and the difference in the adder is placed in A, and AQ is doubled to form a new partial remainder. At each doubling of AQ, q_1 is shifted into q_0 as well as into a_{39}. Thus after 39 steps q_0 has the sign of the quotient. The dividend is used as the initial partial remainder; after 39 quotient digits have been generated, the process is complete. A similar procedure is employed if divisor or dividend is negative or if both are negative.

The Illiac division has the following properties:

(1) A rounded quotient Q is always generated.
    The roundoff is achieved by setting $q_{39} = 1$
    in all cases.

(2) The thirty-ninth partial remainder is left
    in A and is called the residue r. The true
    remainder R corresponding to the rounded quotient
    is related to r approximately as follows:

$$R = r + (2q_0 - 1) y, \qquad (2.4)$$

where y is the divisor and q_0 is the sign

digit of the quotient. Thus if the quotient
is positive

$$R = r - y, \qquad\qquad (2.5)$$

and if the quotient is negative

$$R = r + y. \qquad\qquad (2.6)$$

The equations given above for the true remainder
are valid if the absolute value of the quotient is
less than one, and they yield results in error by
not more than 2^{-39}.

(3) The sign digit of the quotient replaces the least
significant (78th) digit of the double-precision
dividend. One effect is that the least significant
digit of the residue (a_{39}) is the same as the sign
digit of the quotient q_0.

(4) If we have a priori knowledge of the true value q
of the quotient (such as, for example, a division
of qy by y), the relationship between the machine
quotient Q and the true quotient q is

$$Q = q + 2^{-39} (1 - q_{39}) (1 - 2y_0) \qquad (2.7)$$

where q_{39} is the least significant digit of q and
y_0 is the sign digit of the divisor y. Equation
2.7 is essentially a description of the division
roundoff. If $q_{39} = 1$, then $Q = q$ and the machine

2-14

quotient is the true quotient. If $q_{39} = 0$
the nature of the roundoff depends upon the
sign of the divisor. Suppose, for example, that
q is 0.101; then Q is either 0.101000...001 or
0.100111...111 depending upon whether the divisor
was positive or negative, respectively.

2.12   PRECISE CALCULATION OF THE DIVISION REMAINDER.   We
define the remainder R in relation to a quotient Q, a divisor y,
and a dividend d by the equation

$$Qy + 2^{-39} R = d,$$

or

$$R = 2^{39} (d - Qy). \qquad (2.8)$$

However, the exact relationship involving the Illiac residue r and
including the replacement of the least significant dividend digit
d_{78} by the quotient digit q_0 is

$$Qy + 2^{-39} \left[r + (2q_0 - 1)y \right] = d + 2^{-78}(q_0 - d_{78}). \qquad (2.9)$$

Solving for R, we have

$$R = 2^{39} (d - Qy) = r + (2q_0 - 1) y + 2^{-39} (d_{78} - q_0). \qquad (2.10)$$

Equation 2.10 gives the exact expression for the remainder R which
corresponds to the machine quotient Q.

If the remainder $\bar{R}$ corresponding to the true quotient q
is desired, then $\bar{R}$ is defined as

2-15

$$\ddot{R} = 2^{39} (d - qy).$$ (2.11)

The value of $\bar{R}$ is found by substituting equation 2.7 in equation
2.9 and solving for $\bar{R}$, which yields

$$\bar{R} = r + \left[2q_0 - q_{39} - (1 - q_{39}) \, 2y_0\right] y + 2^{-39}(d_{78} - q_0).$$ (2.12)

2.13   THE DIVISION HANGUP.   SPECIAL CASES OF DIVISION.

Circuits are incorporated in the Illiac for stopping the Illiac if
the quotient resulting from a division exceeds one in absolute value.
The sign digit of the quotient is predictable from the signs of divisor
and dividend. The sign digit of the quotient is calculated in the
Illiac by comparing the dividend and divisor arithmetically. Thus,
by sensing the sign digits of quotient, divisor, and dividend, it
is possible to detect the fact that the quotient exceeds one in
absolute value, and stop the Illiac.

The equations derived in Sections 2.10 and 2.11 are valid
only if the absolute value of the dividend is less than the absolute
value of the divisor. When absolute values of dividend and divisor
are equal, the Illiac generates a quotient $-1 + 2^{-39}$ if the dividend
is negative and the divisor is positive. The quotient is $+1 - 2^{-39}$
if dividend and divisor are both negative. If the dividend is
positive and equal to the absolute value of the divisor, the Illiac
will stop. If the divisor is -1, the Illiac generates a quotient
which is the digitwise complement of the dividend, except for the
quotient roundoff.

2-16

2.14   MEMORY TO Q (Order Type 5) AND STORE (Order Type 4)

INSTRUCTIONS.   Instructions are provided in the Illiac for trans-

ferring a number from a specified memory location to the Q register,

and for transferring a number in A to a specified memory location.

The former instruction can be used to transfer the multiplier

to Q before a multiplication; the latter instruction is used to

transfer a result from A to the memory. If a result lies in Q,

(e.g., a division quotient), it can be transferred to the memory

by using two orders; the first is a variant of the add from Q orders

and transfers the number in Q to A and the second is a store order,

transferring the number in A to the memory.

2.15   ILLUSTRATIVE EXAMPLES.

A.   The Leapfrog I Division Test.   In the Leapfrog

I division test the product xy is formed and is then divided by y.

The sum of the quotient in Q and residue in A is formed and stored.

The sum of quotient and residue is then calculated independently

and compared with the sum previously stored.

The value of the machine quotient Q in the quotient regis-

ter after division of xy by y is given by equation 2.7, with q = x.

Thus

$$Q = x + 2^{-39} (1 - x_{39}) (1 - 2y_0).$$

The value of the residue r left in the accumulator is found from

equation 2.12 by setting $\bar{R} = 0$, x = q, and solving for r:

$$r = \left[x_{39} + (1 - x_{39})\, 2y_0 - 2x_0 \right] y + 2^{-39} (x_0 - x_{39}\, y_{39}).$$

The sum $Q + r$, after rearranging terms, is

$$Q + r = x - 2^{-39}\, x_{39}\, y_{39} - x_0\, (y - 2^{-39}) + (1 - x_0)\, y +$$

$$(1 - x_{39})\, (2y_0 - 1)\, (y - 2^{-39}).$$

The independent calculation of $Q + r$ thus consists of forming $x - 2^{-39}\, x_{39}\, y_{39}$ and either adding y or $(-y + 2^{-39})$ depending upon whether x is positive or negative; and finally, if x_{39} is 0, adding or subtracting $(y - 2^{-39})$ depending upon the sign of y.

        B.   The "Double Precision" Division.   It is sometimes convenient to consider a single precision divisor y as exact and form a "double precision" quotient $s + 2^{-39}t$ utilizing the double precision dividend d originally in AQ. The procedure used is as follows:

1. Form d/y, yielding $s + 2^{-39}$ in Q and $r + 2^{-39}s_0$ in A.

2. Shift right, forming $r/2$ in A and $s/2$ in Q.

3. Form $r/2 + y$ leaving T in Q and a residue u in A.

4. Assemble $s + 2^{-39}t$ by setting t_0 (the sign digit of T) to zero, inserting $q/2$ in A and shifting left once.

The precision of $s + 2^{-39}t$ can then be calculated as follows:

        Step 1 yields s and r such that (by equation 2.9)

$$(s + 2^{-39})y + 2^{-39} \left[r + 2^{-39}\, s_0 + (2s_0 - 1)y \right] = d + 2^{-78}(s_0 - d_{78}),$$

or

$$sy + 2^{-39} (r + 2s_0 y) = d - 2^{-78} d_{78}. \qquad (2.13)$$

Step 3 yields

$$Ty + 2^{-39} \left[u + (2t_0 - 1)y \right] = r/2 + 2^{-78} t_0. \qquad (2.14)$$

The following substitutions are made:

(a) $s_0 = t_0$, since the sign of $r/2$ is the same as the sign of d.

(b) From step 4, $t = 2(T + s_0)$ or $T = 1/2t - s_0$.

Substituting in equation 2.14 and solving for r, we have

$$r = (t - 2s_0)y + 2^{-38} \left[u + (2s_0 - 1) \; y \right] - 2^{-77} s_0.$$

Substitution of the value for r in equation 2.13 yields

$$sy + 2^{-39} \left[(t - 2s_0)y + 2s_0 y \right] + 2^{-77} \left[u + 2s_0 - 1)y \right]$$
$$- 2^{-116} s_0 = d - 2^{-78} d_{78}.$$

We thus have

$$(s + 2^{-39}t)y + 2^{-78} \left[2u + 2(2s_0 - 1) \; y + d_{78} - 2^{-38} s_0 \right] = d.$$

It can be shown that $u + (2s_0 - 1) \; y < 1$ so that the quantity within square brackets is less than 3 in absolute value. We conclude that the quotient $s + 2^{-39}t$ is in error by not more than 2^{-76}.

The program for forming a "double precision" quotient

2-19

from a double precision dividend and an exact single precision divisor is given in words 57 to 66 of library routine A4 entitled, "1.7 Precision Floating Decimal". A major difficulty encountered is the formation of r/2 from r (Step 2 above), for r may be as large as 2y and may therefore exceed range. It is therefore necessary to set the sign digit of r/2 to that of the original dividend d.

2.16   <u>INTEGER OPERATIONS.</u>   It is sometimes desirable to use integers for computations in the Illiac. Suppose we have an integer a stored in the memory or arithmetic unit. In terms of the formulation of previous sections, we would store $2^{-39}a$, where a lies in the range $-2^{39} \leq a < 2^{39}$. If we wish to add or subtract two integers a and b, no difficulty is encountered, for $2^{-39}a \pm 2^{-39}b = 2^{-39}(a \pm b)$ indicating that the correct sum or difference lies in A after the instruction is performed. Multiplication of two integers a, b yields $(2^{-39}a)(2^{-39}b) = 2^{-78}ab$. The product ab lies in AQ and is in the range $-2^{78} \leq ab < 2^{78}$. If the programmer scales all quantities so that the product remains in the range $-2^{39} \leq ab < 2^{39}$, then the 40 digit signed product can be transferred to A by a left shift of 39 digital positions. It should be noted that the sign digit of Q is set to zero during the multiplication so that for positive products, $N(Q) = ab$, if $0 \leq ab < 2^{39}$.

Division of integers presents certain difficulties. An example is given here of a method of dividing a positive dividend a by a positive divisor b to yield a quotient f and remainder g.

The steps are as follows:

(1) Place the dividend $2^{-78}a$ in AQ $\quad 0 \leq a < 2^{77}$,

(2) Shift left one digital position, leaving $2a$ in AQ with $q_{39} = 0$,

(3) Divide by $2^{-39}b$, leaving $(2f + 1) 2^{-39}$ in Q and $(2g) 2^{-39}$ in A. $\quad 0 \leq b < 2^{-39}$,

(4) Shift right one digital position, leaving $2^{-39}f$ in Q and $2^{-39}g$ in A.

It can be proved that $bf + g = a$ by substitution of the appropriate quantities in equation 2.9, as follows:

$$(2f + 1) 2^{-39} (2^{-39}b) + 2^{-39} \left[2^{-39}(2g) - 2^{-39}b \right] = 2^{-78}(2a)$$

which yields

$$2^{-78} (2bf + b + 2g - b) = 2^{-78} (2a) \text{ or } bf + g = a.$$

The ranges of f and g are $0 \leq f < 2^{38}$ and $0 \leq g < 2^{38}$.

2.17 <u>SUMMARY.</u> In the Illiac arithmetic unit are two registers, A and Q, which are directly accessible to the programmer. A single arithmetic order of a program utilizes the initial numerical operands in A, in Q, and in a specified memory location, and transforms these quantities to produce desired results which are left in the registers. The programmer must know where the operands are initially located and where the results are to be found. The functions of the registers for the operations of arithmetic are indicated in Table 2.1.

The Illiac has a fixed point arithmetic unit; the binary point is fixed so that any number x used in computation must lie in the range $-1 \leq x < 1$. The programmer must insure that all quantities remain within this range during a computation. The sign of a numerical quantity is indicated by the leftmost of the forty binary digits stored in a register or a memory location. The sign digit is 0 for a positive number 1 for a negative number.

Table 2.1 Use of Illiac Registers During Arithmetic Instructions

TYPE	INSTRUCTION	INITIAL CONDITIONS			FINAL CONDITIONS		NOTES
		Specified Memory Location	A Register	Q Register	A Register	Q Register	
L	Add	Addend	Augend	Arbitrary	Sum	Unchanged	Augend can be set to 0 or 1/2
L	Subtract	Subtrahend	Minuend	Arbitrary	Difference	Unchanged	Minuend can be set to 0 or 1/2
7	Clear Multiply	Multiplicand	Set to 0 at start of instruction	Multiplier	Double Precision Product	Double Precision Product	q_0 set to 0
7	Rounded Multiply	"	Set to 1/2 at start of instruction	"	Rounded Product	Usually Unwanted	"
7	Hold Multiply	" y	Accumulant a	"	$xy + 2^{-39} a$	"	"
6	Divide	Divisor	Double Precision Dividend	Double Precision Dividend	Residue	Rounded Quotient	
0	Left Shift (n 1)	See Note 2	Double Precision Number	x	2x		1. q_0 unchanged 2. Address digits specify number (n) of shifts
1	Right Shift (n 1)	"	"	x	x/2		

2-23

CHAPTER 3

THE ORDER CODE

The Illiac is a binary computer in which the storage
capacity of each register or memory location is 40 binary digits.
The orders which the machine carries out are represented by numbers
in the machine. The relation between the order types and the corresponding numbers is called a code, and the collection of all such
numbers is called the order code of the machine. The order code
is interpreted by the control circuits of the machine and completely
determines what the machine does. The machine is designed so that
any storage location in the memory may be used either for orders or
for numbers, the only distinction being that the control must be in-
structed properly so that orders and numbers will be treated
appropriately.

3.1 THE MAKEUP OF ORDERS. An order for a digital computer
consists of an instruction to say what to do and one or more addresses
to say where to get the quantities to be used in carrying out the instruction. In contrast to some existing computers, the Illiac uses
what is called a one-address code. For a one-address code, the order
is of the kind that says "add the number in memory location 12 to a
number already in the arithmetic unit, leaving the sum in the arithmetic unit".

Since a one-address code is used, it is not necessary to use
40 binary digits to describe an order. The Illiac uses 20 digits and

3-1

packs two orders (an order pair) into one location. These are the
left-hand order and the right-hand order. Since many orders must
refer to locations in the memory, each order contains an address.
It is still called an address in those orders which do not refer
to the memory.

The electrostatic memory of the Illiac has 1024 locations
and because $1024 = 2^{10}$ we require 10 binary digits for the address.
These are the rightmost 10 digits of the 20 digits assigned to an
order.

Of the remaining 10 digits of each order, eight are used
for the instruction or (function) and the other 2 are unused. The
digit makeup of an order pair is shown in Figure 3.1.

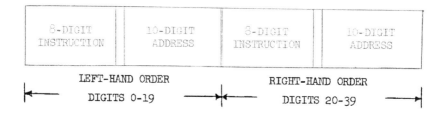

Figure 3.1
Order Pair Makeup

The instruction digits are 8 in number because of the
convenience obtained by using a base 16 (sexadecimal) number system

3-2

in which 4 binary digits may be represented by one sexadecimal digit. Thus each instruction may be coded as 2 sexadecimal digits. The symbols K, S, N, J, F, L are used for 10, 11, 12, 13, 14, 15.

As an example of an order pair, let us consider the following 40 binary digits.

1111010100000001110101000000000000000110

When divided into instruction and address digits, these digits look like this:

1111 0101 00 0000011101   0100 0000 00 0000000110
INSTRUCTION   L.H. ADDRESS INSTRUCTION   R.H. ADDRESS

The left-hand instruction is made up of the two 4-digit numbers 1111 0101 which are the sexadecimal digits L5. The left-hand address is interpreted as an integer which may go from 0 to 1023 if we use decimal notation or from 0 to 3LL if we use sexadecimal notation.

In sexadecimal representation the left hand address is 1J which corresponds to the decimal number 29. Thus the left hand order is L501J where the 0 has been supplied so that all 20 binary digits (including the unused 2) are accounted for. (We could have set the unused digits to 1's and used N rather than 0 if we had wished.)

Similarly the right hand order is 40006, and we have, in sexadecimal notation, the order pair

L501J 40006.

This order pair says, "Transfer the contents of memory location 1J to the accumulator; store the accumulator contents at location 6 of the memory."

It is quite inconvenient to have to write addresses in sexadecimal form, and it is unnecessary if the machine contains a program which will take addresses written in decimal form and convert them to sexadecimal (i.e., binary) form for machine use. A program of this type is available for the Illiac. It is called the Decimal Order Input Routine (See Chapter 5).

3.2 <u>EXECUTION OF ORDERS.</u> The Illiac operates by using orders which have been stored in the memory according to a plan determined by the programmer. The program is begun with a particular order chosen by the programmer. Let us suppose that it is the left hand order at location 10. (We shall refer to addresses in decimal notation.) The control will put into R_3 the order pair from location 10. Then, until something is said to the contrary the control will follow a fixed pattern in executing orders. It will do the left hand order and then the right hand order in R_3. Then it will put the order pair at location 11 into R_3 and again do the left and right hand orders. It will continue to withdraw and execute order pairs from successive memory locations until one of two things occurs:

(a) One of the orders brought out says "stop",

(b) One of the orders brought out says "change the sequencing".

Control Transfer Orders.   The second kind of order, a <u>con-</u>
<u>trol</u> <u>transfer</u> <u>order</u>, permits the programmer to change the sequencing
of orders and provides the flexibility required for iterative processes.
It works in the following way. Let us suppose that after the machine
has executed the left-hand order at location 17 the programmer wishes
to move to a sequence of orders beginning, say, with the right-hand
order at location 35. Then the right-hand order at location 17 will
say "Transfer control to the right-hand order at location 35". The
execution of this order will consist of arranging that the next order
pair is brought to R_3 from location 35 and that the left-hand order
is skipped. Having done the right-hand order in R_3, the control brings
out the order pair from location 36 and proceeds in the usual way.

Conditional Transfer Orders.   There are two kinds of con-
trol transfer orders, <u>conditional</u> <u>transfer</u> <u>orders</u> and <u>unconditional</u>
<u>transfer</u> <u>orders</u>. We have just described the unconditional transfer
order. The conditional transfer order does the same thing as the
unconditional transfer order <u>provided</u> <u>that</u> <u>the</u> <u>number</u> <u>in</u> <u>the</u> accumulator <u>is</u> <u>not</u> <u>negative</u>. Otherwise it does nothing. In the example
we have just used, if the right-hand order at location 17 had been
conditional, then if the accumulator had held zero or a positive
number the next order executed would have been the right hand order
at location 35. But if the accumulator had held a negative number
the next order executed would have been the left hand order at location
18.

3.3 __STOP ORDERS.__ There are four control transfer orders, the right-hand and left-hand unconditional and conditional orders. These have been further combined with a stop or not-stop order, giving eight orders in all. If the programmer chooses one of the four "stop and transfer control" orders the machine will stop before transferring control and must be started again with a panel switch. The switch can be set so that these stop orders are ignored, which of course makes these stop orders into ordinary control transfer orders. This is often useful in programming, and when it is done the machine can still be stopped with another kind of stop order which cannot be ignored.

3.4 __ORDER TYPES.__ The number of orders which the Illiac can execute is quite large (more than 100), but not all of them are of general interest. What we shall do here is discuss the various types of orders, giving the variants of each. Following this discussion will be a list of those Illiac orders which are of most use. This list is adequate for the coding of any problem, and beginners are urged to confine themselves to it. Experienced coders will find uses for other variants.

The two sexadecimal instruction digits of an order give the order _type_ and the order _variant_. We shall refer to them as the T- and V- digits, respectively. In the example L5 cited earlier the T- digit is L and denotes addition. The V- digit is 5 and chooses one of the variants of the addition order.

3-6

The order types are given in Table 3.1.

T-Digit	Order Type
0	Left Shift
1	Right Shift
2	Unconditional Transfer
3	Conditional Transfer
4	Store from A register
5	Memory to Q register
6	Divide
7	Multiply
8	Input or Output
9	Special Input or Output
K	Increment Add from Q
S	Add from Q register
N	Not Used
J	Extract
F	Increment Add
L	Add

Table 3.1
Order Types

The meaning of the address digits of the different order
types given in Table 3.2.

ORDER-TYPE	ADDRESS SIGNIFICANCE
0, 1	Number of shifts (cannot exceed 63)
2, 3	Memory location from which next order pair will come
4	Memory location at which storage will occur
5	Memory location from which word is brought to Q register
6	Memory location of divisor
7	Memory location of multiplicand
80, 82	Number of binary digits to be input or output
92	Character to be punched and number of punchings
K, S	Address not used
J	Same as for 5 order
F	Memory location of addend
L	Memory location of addend

Table 3.2

Meaning of Address Digits

It will be seen from Table 3.2 that except for the 0, 1, 8, 9, K and S orders the address of an order always refers to the memory.

3.5   ORDER VARIANTS.   Let us now consider the variants obtained by changing the V-digit. The sexadecimal V-digit is made up of the four binary digits V8, V4, V2 and V1. There are 16 possible combinations, giving V-digits from 0 to L, but not all are used. The results obtained with different V-digits are as follows:

(a)   The Digit V1.   If V1 = 1, A will always be cleared to zero at the beginning of any order. If V1 = 0, A will not be cleared. Thus an odd V-digit means that A will be cleared.

(b)   The Digit V8.   If V1 = 1 and V8 = 1, the quantity 1/2 will be put in A at the beginning of any order. This is how rounded multiplication is carried out. If V8 =1 and V1 = 0, the Illiac will hang up.

(c)   The Digit V2.   This digit affects all orders except those of types 0, 1, 5 and J. See Table 3.3

(d)   The Digit V4.   This digit affects all orders except those of types 0, 1, 5 and J. See Table 3.3.

The following notation is convenient for a more detailed description of the orders:

A = accumulator register

a_o = sign digit of A

Q = multiplier-quotient register

q_o = sign digit of Q

AQ = the 79 binary digit double register formed from A and Q by omitting q_o.

$N(R)$ = contents of register R

$N(n)$ = contents of memory location n

If no ambiguity is possible, the symbols A and Q will also be used to denote the contents of A and of Q.

On the following pages there are detailed descriptions of
the results obtained by changing the V-digit of the 15 order types
used in the Illiac. After the detailed descriptions is an abbreviated list of orders. The orders in the abbreviated list have been
underlined in the detailed descriptions.

Table 3.3 Effect of Digits V4 and V2

TYPE	V4	EFFECT OF V4	V2	EFFECT OF V2
0, 1	--	NONE	--	NONE
2, 3	0 / 1	RIGHT-HAND ORDER / LEFT-HAND ORDER	0 / 1	STOP IF SWITCH SET TO OBEY NONE
4	--	NONE	0	STORE FULL WORD
			1	STORE ADDRESS
5, 3	0 / 1	RIGHT-HAND ADDRESS / LEFT-HAND ADDRESS	--	NONE
6	1	V4 MUST BE 1	1	V2 MUST BE 1
8	0 / 1	TAPE / DRUM	0 / 1	INPUT / OUTPUT
9	0	TAPE	0 / 1	INPUT / OUTPUT
7, K, S F, L	0 / 1	SUBTRACT ADD	0 / 1	NUMBER ABSOLUTE VALUE

OV n   Left Shift (Double)   3 Orders
                            Final Stop   1 Order

If n = 0, the machine will stop. If not, repeat n times
the operation which replaces the contents

$$a_0, a_1, a_2, \cdots, a_{38}, a_{39}; q_1, q_2, q_3, \cdots, q_{38}, q_{39}$$

of AQ by

$$a_1, a_2, a_3, \cdots, a_{39} q_1; q_2, q_3, q_4, \cdots, q_{39}, 0$$

leaving q_0 unchanged.

The number n will be interpreted modulo 64.

Variants

0, 2, 4, 6   Order as described above.

1, 3, 5, 7   Clear A and then execute as described.

8, K, N   Illiac will hang up. Avoid these.

9, S, J, L   Clear A, insert 1/2 in A, and then execute
                order as described above.

F   Final Stop.

Use only 00, 01, 09 for shifts
Use OF with n = 0 for final stop

If n = 0, the machine will stop. If not, repeat n times the operation which replaces the contents

$$a_0, a_1, a_2, \cdots, a_{38}, a_{39}; q_1, q_2, q_3, \cdots, q_{38}, q_{39}$$

of AQ by

$$a_0, a_0, a_1, \cdots, a_{37}, a_{38}; a_{39}, q_1, q_2, \cdots, q_{37}, q_{38},$$

leaving q_0 unchanged.

The number n will be interpreted modulo 64.

Variants

0, 2, 4, 6	Order as described above.
1, 3, 5, 7	Clear A and then execute as described.
8, K, N, F	Illiac will hang up. Avoid these.
9, S, J, L	Clear A, insert 1/2 in A, and then execute order as described above.

Use only 10, 11, 19

Bring the next order pair from memory location n and

choose the left or right hand order of this pair, stopping before-

hand or not, depending upon V.

Variants

0	Stop. The first order after starting with the START switch will be the <u>right</u> <u>hand</u> order at memory location n. The stop can be ignored by setting a panel switch.
2	Transfer control to <u>right</u> <u>hand</u> order at memory location.
4	Same as 0 except take <u>left</u> <u>hand</u> order.
6	Same as 2 except take <u>left</u> <u>hand</u> order.
1, 3, 5, 7	Same as 0, 2, 4, 6 except clear A first.
8, K, N, F	Illiac will hang up. Avoid these.
9, S, J, L	Same as 1, 3, 5, 7 except also make A = 1/2 after clearing.

Use <u>20</u>, 21, <u>22</u>, 23, <u>24</u>, 25, <u>26</u>, 27, 29, 2S, 2J, 2L.

Starting After A Stop. When the Illiac has been stopped

by one of the control transfer stop orders, it is usually started

again by moving the black switch to START, from which position the

switch automatically returns to OBEY.

The Illiac can also be started again by moving the white

switch through EXECUTE to FETCH and then back to RUN. If this is done, the control transfer order which stopped the Illiac will be ignored. The normal sequencing will then follow unless the stop order is a right hand order transferring control to the right hand side of a word. In this case, the order first obeyed after starting will be the right hand instead of the left hand order of the new order pair brought out.

For example consider the following orders:

p	L5	F
	20	p+2
p+1	40	1F
	24	p
p+2	7J	2F
	L4	3F

If we stop with the 20 order, the black switch will start with L4 3F and the white switch with 24 p. If we stop with the 24 order, the black switch will start with L5 F and the white switch with 7J 2F.

If A $\geq$ 0, bring the next order pair from memory location
n and choose the left or right hand order of this pair, stopping be-
forehand or not, depending upon V.   If A $<$ 0, go on to the next
order.

Variants

0, 2, 4, 6	If A $\geq$ 0, do the same operation as for the corresponding 2V order. If A $<$ 0, go on to the next order.
1, 3, 5, 7	Identical with corresponding 2V orders.
8, K, N, F	Illiac will hang up. Avoid these.
9, S, J, L	Identical with corresponding 2V orders.

Use only 30, 32, 34, 36.

Starting After A Stop.   The discussion given with the
2V orders applies here to the corresponding 3V orders.

Copy into memory location n all of the contents of A,
the contents corresponding to the address of a left hand order, or
the contents corresponding to the address of a right hand order,
depending upon V.

Variants

0, 4   Replace N(n) by A.

1, 5   Replace N(n) and A by 0.

2   Replace address digits of <u>right hand</u> order
            at memory location n by the corresponding
            digits of A.

3   Same as 2 except clear A first.

6   Same as 2 except take <u>left hand</u> order.

8, K, N, F Illiac will hang up. Avoid these.

9, J   Replace N(n) and A by 1/2.

S   Replace A by 1/2 and address digits of
            <u>right hand</u> order at memory location n
            by 0.

L   Same as S except take <u>left hand</u> order.

Use only 4̲0̲, 4̲1̲, 4̲2̲, 43, 4̲6̲, 47, 4̲9̲, 4S, 4L.

Transfer N(n) to Q

Variants

0, 2, 4, 6   Transfer N(n) to Q

1, 3, 5, 7   Clear A and transfer N(n) to Q.

8, K, N, F   Illiac will hang up. Avoid these.

9, S, J, L   Put 1/2 in A and transfer N(n) to Q.

Use only 50, 51, 59.

Divide AQ by N(n), placing the rounded quotient in Q (the least significant digit being 1 for the roundoff) and leaving a residue in A.   If $\left|A\right| > \left|N(n)\right|$ the Illiac will stop after dividing. If $|A| = \left|N(n)\right|$ and if $A \geq 0$, the Illiac will stop after dividing; if $\left|A\right| = \left|N(n)\right|$ and if $A < 0$, the Illiac will not stop after dividing.

Variants

6	As described above.
7	Make A = 0, then proceed as above.
L, S	Make A = 1/2, then proceed as above.
8, K, N, F	Illiac will hang up. Avoid these.
0, 1, 2, 3 4, 5, 9, J	These give incorrect results or results which are correct only under certain conditions. Avoid them.

Use only <u>66</u>, 67, 6L.

Put $Q \times P(n) + 2^{-39} A$ into AQ, the least significant 39 digits being in Q with $q_0 = 0$.

Variants

0	$P(n) = - N(n)$
1	$P(n) = - N(n); A=0$
2	$P(n) = - \lvert N(n) \rvert$
3	$P(n) = - \lvert N(n) \rvert \; ; A=0$
4	$P(n) = N(n)$
5	$P(n) = N(n); A=0$
6	$P(n) = \lvert N(n) \rvert$
7	$P(n) = \lvert N(n) \rvert \; ; A=0$
8, K, N, F	Illiac will hang up. Avoid these.
9	$P(n) = - N(n); A = 1/2$
S	$P(n) = - \lvert N(n) \rvert ; A = 1/2$
J	$P(n) = N(n); A = 1/2$
L	$P(n) = \lvert N(n) \rvert ; A = 1/2$

Use only 70, 71, 72, 73, 74, 75,
76, 77, 79, 7S, 7J, 7L.

Transfer words between A and the input tape, output punch, or magnetic drum.

The address n must be a multiple of 4 for the tape and punch orders and must be 11 for drum orders.

Variants

0	Shift AQ four places left as in the 00 order and replace a_{36}, a_{37}, a_{38}, a_{39} by the binary digits corresponding to the sexadecimal character being read. This is done $n/4$ times.
1,9	Clear A and then do as in 80 order.
2	Punch the digits a_0, a_1, a_2, a_3 as one sexa-decimal character and shift AQ four places left as in the 00 order. This is done $n/4$ times.
3	Clear A and do as in 82 order.
5	This is a 40-digit order of the form 85 11 T v̄ p. We distinguish two cases.
	(1) T is not 0, 1, 8, 9. In this case, A and Q are shifted left eleven places as in the 00 order and the word at drum location p is placed in A. Then the T order is executed using address p. Complete freedom is not available in drum addresses because p may interfere with V.

	(2) T is 0, 1, 8, 9. In this case after the word at drum location p is placed in A the right hand order is skipped. This permits use of any drum address for p.
6	This is a 40-digit order of the form 85 11 TV p. We again have two cases:
	(1) T is not 0, 1, 8, 9. In this case A is transferred to drum location p, and A and Q are shifted 11 places left as in the 00 order. Then the T order is executed using address p. Complete freedom is not available in drum addresses because p may interfere with V.
	(2) T is 0, 1, 8, 9. In this case the right hand order is skipped after doing the left hand order as in case (1). This permits use of any drum address p.
7	Same as 86 except clear A first.
S	Put 1/2 in A and do as in 82 order.
L	Put 1/2 in A and do as in 86 order.
8, K, N, F	Illiac will hang up. Avoid these.
4, J	These are not useful. Avoid them.

Use 80, 81, 82, 83, 85, 86, 87, 8S, 8L.

Variants

1   Five hole input. Shift AQ four places <u>right</u> and re-place a_{36}, a_{37}, a_{38}, a_{39} by the binary digits corre-sponding to the four least significant holes on the tape. Place the contents of the fifth hole in posi-tion a_0.

2   Letter output. Punch on the tape a character de-pending upon the address digits n. Three quantities are defined by the 10 binary address digits:

(1)   The leftmost 4 digits define the usual 4 digit positions in the output tape.

(2)   The rightmost digit defines the 5th hole in the output tape.

(3)   The rightmost 6 digits determine the number b of times that the above-defined character is punched and also the number of <u>right</u> <u>shifts</u> executed. The number of characters punched will be found by dividing the number in the rightmost 6 digits by 4 and <u>rounding</u> <u>up</u> to the next integer.

The address n may always be found from the following formula:

$$n = 64a + 4b + c - 2$$

where a is the character punched, $a = 0, 1, 2, \ldots, J, F, L$

      b   is the number of characters punched, $1 \leq b \leq 16$

      c   determines the fifth hole, $c = 0, 1$.

The number of right shifts executed is $4b + c - 2$.

Example.   Punch the character 7 thirteen times.

$$n = 64 \times 7 + 4 \times 13 + 0 - 2 = 498$$

It will be found that the last 6 digits contain the number 50 which when divided by 4 and rounded up gives 13.   There will be 50 right shifts.

Figure 3.2 shows the relationship between the tape holes and the address digits of the 92 order.   The address shown will print the character 7 thirteen times.

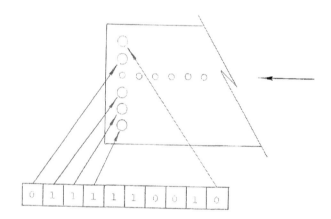

Figure 3.2

Address Digits of 92 Order

3-24

These orders are identical with the FV orders except that Q is used instead of N(n).

Variants

0	Add $-Q - 2^{-39}$ to A. (See note).
1	Put $-Q - 2^{-39}$ in A.
2	Same as 0 if $Q \geq 0$; same as 4 if $Q < 0$.
3	Same as 1 if $Q \geq 0$; same as 5 if $Q < 0$.
4	Add $Q + 2^{-39}$ to A.
5	Put $Q + 2^{-39}$ to A.
6	Same as 4 if $Q \geq 0$; same as 0 if $Q < 0$.
7	Same as 5 if $Q \geq 0$; same as 1 if $Q < 0$.
8, K, N, F	Illiac will hang up. Avoid these.
9	Put $-Q - 2^{-39} + 1/2$ in A.
S	Same as 9 if $Q \geq 0$; same as J if $Q < 0$.
J	Put $Q + 2^{-39} + 1/2$ in A.
L	Same as J if $Q \geq 0$; same as 9 if $Q < 0$.

Use K0, K1, K3, K4, K5, K6, K7, K9, KS, KJ, KL

NOTE: $- Q - 2^{-39}$ is the digitwise complement of Q.

Q is added, subtracted, etc., to A. These orders are identical with the LV orders with Q used instead of N(n).

Variants

0	Subtract Q from A.
1	Put -Q in A.
2	Subtract $\|Q\|$ from A.
3	Put - $\|Q\|$ in A.
4	Add Q to A.
5	Put Q in A.
6	Add $\|Q\|$ to A.
7	Put $\|Q\|$ in A.
8, K, N, F	Illiac will hang up. Avoid these.
9	Put 1/2 - Q in A.
S	Put 1/2 - $\|Q\|$ in A.
J	Put 1/2 + Q in A.
L	Put 1/2 + $\|Q\|$ in A.

Use S0, S1, S2, S3, S4, S5, S6, S7, S9, SS, SJ, SL

If two corresponding digits of N(n) and Q are both
1's, put 1 in that place of Q. Otherwise put 0. This order gives
the logical product of N(n) and Q.

Variants

0, 2, 4, 6	As described above.
1, 3, 5, 7	Clear A and do J0 order.
8, K, N, F	Illiac will hang up. Avoid these.
9, S, J, L	Put 1/2 in A and do J0 order.

Use only J0, J1, J9.

<u>Variants</u>

0	Add $-N(n) - 2^{-39}$ to A. (See note)
1	Put $-N(n) - 2^{-39}$ in A.
2	Same as 0 if $N(n) \geq 0$; same as 4 if $N(n) < 0$.
3	Same as 1 if $N(n) \geq 0$; same as 5 if $N(n) < 0$.
4	Add $N(n) + 2^{-39}$ to A.
5	Put $N(n) + 2^{-39}$ in A.
6	Same as 4 if $N(n) \geq 0$; same as 0 if $N(n) < 0$.
7	Same as 5 if $N(n) \geq 0$; same as 1 if $N(n) < 0$.
8, K, N, F	Illiac will hang up. Avoid these.
9	Put $-N(n) - 2^{-39} + 1/2$ in A.
S	Same as 9 if $N(n) \geq 0$; same as J if $N(n) < 0$.
J	Put $N(n) + 2^{-39} + 1/2$ in A.
L	Same as J if $N(n) \geq 0$; same as 9 if $N(n) < 0$.

Use F0, <u>F1</u>, F2, F3, <u>F4</u>, <u>F5</u>, F6, F7, F9, FS, FJ, FL.

NOTE: $-N(n) - 2^{-39}$ is the digitwise complement of $N(n)$.

$N(n)$ is added, subtracted, etc., to A.

Variants

0	Subtract $N(n)$ from A.
1	Put $-N(n)$ in A.
2	Subtract $|N(n)|$ from A.
3	Put $-|N(n)|$ in A.
4	Add $N(n)$ to A.
5	Put $N(n)$ in A.
6	Add $|N(n)|$ to A.
7	Put $|N(n)|$ in A.
8, K, N, F	Illiac will hang up. Avoid these.
9	Put $1/2 - N(n)$ in A.
S	Put $1/2 - |N(n)|$ in A.
J	Put $1/2 + N(n)$ in A.
L	Put $1/2 + |N(n)|$ in A.

Use L0, L1, L2, L3, L4, L5, L6, L7, L9, LS, LJ, LL.

ABBREVIATED ORDER LIST

ORDER	DESCRIPTION

00 n   Shift AQ left n places, $1 \leq n \leq 63$.

09 n   Make A = 1/2 and then shift AQ left n places, $1 \leq n \leq 63$.

OF 0   Final stop.

10 n   Shift AQ right n places, $1 \leq n \leq 63$.

19 n   Make A = 1/2 and shift AQ right n places so that AQ contains 2^{-n-1}, $1 \leq n \leq 63$.

20 n   Stop. The first order after START will be the right hand order at location n. The stop can be ignored by setting the panel switch to IGNORE.

22 n   Transfer control to the right hand order at location n.

24 n   Same as 20 except take left hand order.

26 n   Same as 22 except take left hand order.

30 n

32 n   If $A \geq 0$ do as in the corresponding 2V order.

34 n   If $A < 0$ go on to the next order.

36 n

40 n   Replace N(n) by A. Do not change A.

41 n   Replace N(n) and A by zero.

ORDER	DESCRIPTION
42 n	Replace address digits of the right hand order at location n by the corresponding digits of A. Do not change A.
46 n	Replace address digits of the left hand order at location n by the corresponding digits of A. Do not change A.
49 n	Replace $N(n)$ and A by $1/2$.
50 n	Replace Q by $N(n)$.
66 n	Divide $A + 2^{-39} (Q + q_0)$ by $N(n)$.
70 n	Put $-N(n) Q + 2^{-39} A$ into AQ.
71 n	Multiply $-N(n)$ by Q, putting result in AQ.
72 n	Put $- \|N(n)\| Q + 2^{-39} A$ into AQ.
73 n	Multiply $- \|N(n)\|$ by Q, putting result in AQ.
74 n	Put $N(n) Q + 2^{-39} A$ into AQ.
75 n	Multiply $N(n)$ by Q, putting result in AQ.
76 n	Put $\|N(n)\| Q + 2^{-39} A$ into AQ.
77 n	Multiply $\|N(n)\|$ by Q, putting result in AQ.
79 n	Put the rounded product $-N(n) Q$ into A.
7S n	Put the rounded product $- \|N(n)\| Q$ into A.
7J n	Put the rounded product $N(n) Q$ into A.
7L n	Put the rounded product $\|N(n)\| Q$ into A.
80 n	Input $n/4$ sexadecimal characters from the tape.
81 n	Clear A and input $n/4$ sexadecimal characters from the tape.

ORDER	DESCRIPTION
82 n	Punch n/4 sexadecimal characters on the tape.
85 n.	Replace A by the word at drum location n. See page 3-21.
86 n	Replace the word at drum location n by A. See page 3-22.
91 4	Read one five-hole character from the tape.
92 1	Close shutter.
92 131	Punch one carriage return and line feed character.
92 642	Punch one + sign (or K).
92 706	Punch one - sign (or S).
92 769	Advance film and open shutter.
92 963	Punch one space character.
K1 n	Put $- Q - 2^{-39}$ in A. (This is the digitwise complement of Q).
K4 n	Add $Q + 2^{-39}$ to A.
K5 n	Put $Q + 2^{-39}$ in A.
S0 n	Subtract Q from A.
S1 n	Put $- Q$ in A.
S2 n	Subtract $|Q|$ from A.
S3 n	Put $-|Q|$ in A.
S4 n	Add Q to A.
S5 n	Put Q in A.
S6 n	Add $|Q|$ to A.
S7 n	Put $|Q|$ in A

ORDER	DESCRIPTION
JO n	Replace Q by the logical product of Q and $N(n)$.
F1 n	Put $-N(n) - 2^{-39}$ in A. (This is the digit-wise complement of $N(n)$).
F4 n	Add $N(n) + 2^{-39}$ to A.
F5 n	Put $N(n) + 2^{-39}$ in A.
L0 n	Subtract $N(n)$ from A.
L1 n	Put $- N(n)$ in A.
L2 n	Subtract $|N(n)|$ from A.
L3 n	Put $- |N(n)|$ in A.
L4 n	Add $N(n)$ to A.
L5 n	Put $N(n)$ in A.
L6 n	Add $|N(n)|$ to A.
L7 n	Put $|N(n)|$ in A.

CHAPTER 4

ROUTINES

One of the first tasks in programming a computation is to break it down into a number of small or medium size operations, each of which forms a fairly distinct logical step in the whole calculation. Such a step may be the evaluation of a function such as a square root, logarithm or cosine. Each step must be carefully defined so that it fits correctly with all the other steps. Having decided exactly what is required of each step, it is possible to proceed with the coding of the individual steps.

This procedure has three important advantages. Firstly, it enables the programmer to concentrate on one part of the job at a time. Secondly, the coding of each step can be tested separately before incorporating it in the program. Thirdly, certain steps are common to a very large number of different calculations; these have been coded and tested once for all, and may be used by any one in the laboratory.

The coding for one step constitutes a _routine._ The collection of routines for performing common operations in the Illiac is called the _library_ of routines. It includes routines for evaluating many simple functions like those mentioned above, also for printing numbers in various layouts, for integrating differential equations, for solving simultaneous equations, and for many other operations.

4-1

A routine, when used to perform part of the work of another routine, is called a subroutine. The simplest type of subroutine is merely a string of order pairs which can be inserted in the appropriate place among the other orders of a program. This is called an open subroutine. However, for various reasons another type, called a closed subroutine, is more commonly used

4.1 CLOSED SUBROUTINES. A closed subroutine is also a string of consecutive words but these do not have to be placed among the other orders of the program. Instead, they may be put in any convenient place in the store. Each time the subroutine is to be executed, control must be transferred to it in a certain special way (the subroutine is said to be entered). It is so arranged that when execution is complete, control is automatically returned to the point from which the subroutine was entered, so that execution of the rest of the program may continue.

In this way a program is seen to consist of several distinct, self-contained blocks, namely the various subroutines and the part of the program (usually called the main program or master routine) which makes use of its subroutines by sending control to them. Internal rearrangement of a routine is usually difficult, but the routines comprising a program can be shuffled about very easily, and this fact makes the coding of large problems much simpler.

It is not necessary to enter each subroutine directly from the master routine; there is nothing to prevent one subroutine being entered from another. A subroutine may itself have subroutines.

4.2 ENTERING A CLOSED SUBROUTINE. The following two
orders must be inserted in the master routine at the point from which
a subroutine is required to be entered. .

```
        k       Any
                50 k
        k+1     26 m        Subroutine starts at m.
                Any
```

These orders must be, as shown, in the right-hand half of one word
and the left-hand half of the next (it may be necessary to waste an
order to do this). The 50 order contains the address of the memory
location in which it is itself contained. The 26 order contains the
address of the memory location containing the first word of the subroutine (it actually transfers control to the left-hand half of this
word).

     The subroutine, after execution, automatically transfers
control to the order following these, i.e., to the right-hand order
in memory location (k+1), so that there is no break in the logical
continuity of the master routine. There is no need for the user to
know how the subroutine does this, but it is not difficult to under-
stand and it helps to complete the picture.

4.3 RETURNING CONTROL TO THE MASTER ROUTINE. It will
be seen that the effect of the 50 order above is to place the order-
pair, of which it is the right-hand half, in the Q register. Thus
whenever a closed subroutine is entered, the Q register contains a
pair of orders of which the right-hand order contains the address

of the memory location from which the pair came. Control must be returned to the right-hand order in the memory location following this.

The subroutine uses the information in the Q register to set the address in a transfer of control order (a 22 order) called the link, which ultimately causes the transfer back to the master routine. It does this by means of the orders shown in Table 4.1.

m	K5	0	These orders "plant"
	42	m+n	the link
m+1	..	..	
	..	..	
...	..	..	
	..	..	
m+n	..	..	
	22	(0)	link

Table 4.1

Forming a Closed Subroutine Link

The K5 order transfers the order-pair from the Q register to the A register, increasing the right-hand address by 1 as it does so. This address is now the address to which control is eventually to be returned. The 42 order places this address in the link. The link is situated so that it will be encountered by control when the execution of the subroutine is complete. Note that the link should be a right-hand order so that its address may be inserted from the right-hand side of the A register.

It may sometimes be convenient to use a 32 order as a link;

this order may then perform a test within the subroutine and return control to the master routine only if some condition is satisfied. Also the above procedure for "planting" the link may be varied if desired, so long as the result is the same. In particular note the variants in sections 4.5 and 4.6 below.

4.4   PLACING THE ARGUMENT.   All subroutines operate on at least one number somewhere in the machine, and there must be agreement between the subroutine and the master routine on the placing of these numbers, and also on the placing of the results of the subroutine operation.

If only one number is operated upon, it is convenient to use the A register to hold this number when the subroutine is entered (since the A register is not being used for anything else at this moment). Similarly, if only one number is produced by the subroutine it is convenient for the subroutine to leave this number in the A register.

For example, Library Routine R1 is a closed subroutine that finds the square root of the number given in A, and leaves this square root in A. Suppose we wish the Illiac to find the largest root of

$$x^4 + 2x^3 + x^2 - c = 0,$$

where $c = N(10)$ and satisfies $0 \le c \le 1/2$. It can be shown that the root is

$$x = -1/2 + \sqrt{1/4 + \sqrt{c}} \quad .$$

4-5

Suppose that the constants 1/2 and 1/4 are given in 20 and 21 respectively, and that x is required in 11. Routine R1 will be used to find the square roots; let its first word be in 100. Then the master routine might contain the orders of Table 4.2

50	L5	10	Put c in A
	50	50	Enter Code R1
51	26	100	to form $\sqrt{c}$
	L4	21	Add 1/4 to $\sqrt{c}$
52	22	52	Waste order
	50	52	Enter Code R1
53	26	100	to form $\sqrt{1/4 + \sqrt{c}}$
	L0	20	Subtract 1/2 to form x
54	40	11	Put x in 11

Table 4.2

Master Routine Using A Closed Subroutine

The subroutine itself must use a slightly different method of link planting from that given in section 4.3, which would destroy the argument in A before using it. It is here necessary to rescue the argument and hold it in a storage location until the link has been planted, as in Table 4.3

m	40	2	Put argument in q
	K5	0	
m+1	42	m+n	Plant link
	..	..	
m+n	..	..	
	22	(0)	Link

Table 4.3

Modified Link Planting

4.5   PROGRAM PARAMETERS.   Sometimes a subroutine is made to carry out slightly different operations on different occasions. For example, one subroutine might be made to print numbers to any number of figures. Another might form the nth root of a number, where n is any positive integer. The value of n, or the number of figures to be printed, is called a parameter of the subroutine.

The value of a parameter must always be specified if the subroutine is to operate correctly. There are two standard ways of specifying parameters; parameters specified in the way now to be described are called program parameters. (The others are called "preset" parameters - see below, section 4.7).

A program parameter is specified in the first half of the word containing the 50 order which is required on entering any closed subroutine. Let us take for example Library Routine R2, which is a closed subroutine for replacing N(A) by its pth root. Here p is a program parameter, to be specified as follows:

k	50 p	Program parameter
	50 k	
k+1	26 m	Subroutine starts at m
	Any	

To illustrate this, suppose we wish the machine to compute the positive real root of

$$x^6 - 3x^4 + 3x^2 + 2c = 0, \quad (1/2 < c < 1)$$

which is given by the formula

$$x = \div \sqrt{1 + \sqrt[3]{1 - 2c}} \ .$$

4.7

Suppose that c = N(10) and that x is required in 11; suppose also
that N(20) = -1, and that Routine R2 starts at 100. Then the master
routine might contain the program given in Table 4.4

50	L9	10	$N(A) = (1/2) -c$
	00	1	$N(A) = 1 - 2c$
51	50	3	Program parameter
	50	51	Link
52	26	100	To Routine R2
	LO	20	$N(A) = 1 + \sqrt[3]{1 - 2c}$
53	50	2	Program parameter
	50	53	Link
54	26	100	To Routine R2
	40	11	x to 11

Table 4.4

Use of Program Parameter

It will be noticed in Table 4.4 that the order containing the parameter (50 3 or 50 2) is actually obeyed by the machine
before the subroutine is entered. This is just a waste of time
which is not worth avoiding; it does no good and, provided the order
containing the parameter is suitably chosen, no harm. It is usual
to use a 50 order here; this puts rubbish in the Q register, but
the latter is then immediately reset by the following 50 order and
no damage has been done.

A more elaborate example of the use of a program parameter
is to be found in Library Routine P1 which prints A as an integer
or fraction. The entry is by means of the orders of Table 4.5

4-8

k	XY	d
	50	k
k+1	26	m

Table 4.5

Multiple Program Parameters

In Table 4.5 x = 5 or J; if x = 5 and A is negative the printed
number is preceded by a minus sign, otherwise it is preceded by a
space. Also Y = 0 or 2; if Y = 0, A x 2^{39} is printed as an integer;
if Y = 2, A is printed as a fraction (correctly rounded off). The
layout of digits is given by d = 10q + s; q digits are printed with
a space after the first s.

It will be noted that all combinations of X and Y form
harmless orders.

4.6 <u>INTERPRETIVE ROUTINES.</u> There is a type of subroutine which, instead of executing a single distinctive operation,
carries out a whole series of operations. Each operation requires
a parameter for its specification, so that the master routine contains
a string of parameters, one for each operation. The string may be
of indefinite length.

Such subroutines are called interpretive routines. Their
use lies in programs that involve actual operations on elements which
are not numbers stored in the usual form but may be numbers stored
in some special form, or different mathematical entities altogether
such as expansions in Boolean algebra. The commonest application
is to numbers stored in the so-called "floating point" form (see
Chapter 6). There are certain advantages in storing numbers in this

4-9

form; however, such numbers cannot be added or multiplied in a single Illiac operation. A routine is required to handle simple arithmetic, and for this purpose an interpretive routine is used (e.g. Routine A1). Each parameter of the interpretive routine corresponds to one arithmetical operation, just as each Illiac order corresponds to one operation in the Illiac. Thus, for example, to place in register 6 the sum of the numbers in registers 4 and 5 we write the parameters

$$85 \quad 4$$
$$84 \quad 5$$
$$8S \quad 6,$$

which act in a similar way to the Illiac orders

$$L5 \quad 4$$
$$L4 \quad 5$$
$$40 \quad 6.$$

Owing to the close similarity between the parameters and the ordinary Illiac orders, the parameters are themselves often referred to as interpretive orders, or merely as orders, "orders", or orders. The "order code" of the interpretive routine may be described in a similar way to the order code of the machine; it involves reference to an "accumulator" which behaves, for floating point numbers, like the A register of the Illiac.

An interpretive routine is entered in the same way as a closed subroutine, but the parameters (i.e., the interpretive "orders") follow the orders causing entry. Finally a special parameter may be used to cause control to the Illiac to be transferred out of the interpretive routine and back to the master routine. Thus if we

4-10

imagine that the above example is a complete set of operations to
be carried out by the interpretive routine, the master routine
would contain the program of Table 4.6

k	Any		
	50	k	Enter interpretive routine
k+1	26	m	
	85	4	Parameters (interpretive orders)
k+2	84	5	
	8s	6	
k+3	8J	k+4	Send control of Illiac to L. H.
	00	0	side of k+4
	etc.		

Table 4.6
Program for Interpretive Routine

4.7   PRESET PARAMETERS.   By making use of a library
routine a programmer avoids not only the necessity of writing out
the orders, but also the labor of punching them, since a master copy
of the tape is kept on file in the Teletype Room to be copied when
required.

If the routine has one or more parameters associated with
it, it can meet a wide variety of requirements. However, the use
of program parameters consumes both computing time and storage space.

A program parameter has the property that it can be varied
from one application to another within the same program. Frequently
it happens that, although the ability to choose a value of a parameter to suit any particular program is desired, the ability to change

4-11

the value during the execution of a program is not needed. The
value can be set before execution begins; there is no need for the
orders which, in the case of a program parameter, set the value
afresh each time the routine is entered. A parameter whose value
is set before execution begins is called a preset parameter.

The master copy of a library routine must be valid for
all values of any preset parameters involved. The fixing of a pre-
set parameter for a particular program must therefore be done after
(or during) the copying of the master tape; in fact it is done as
the program is read into the Illiac. This operation is carried
out by the Decimal Order Input Routine which is described in
Chapter 5.

CHAPTER 5

THE DECIMAL ORDER INPUT

The Illiac is a binary machine intended for University research. Since it will be used by a large group of people with various scientific backgrounds, it is important that its use be made as simple as possible. To this end a library of subroutines has been organized and aids in using it have been devised. One of these aids is the Decimal Order Input, Library Code X1. This code has two principal purposes:

(1) To make it possible for programmers to use decimal notation in coding,

(2) To make use of the library easy.

The use of subroutines is discussed more fully in Chapter 4, but one way to characterize a subroutine is to say that it is essentially an extension of the order code of the machine. It is a group of orders used to carry out one or more operations which may be as simple as a square root or as complicated as a complete program for executing the details of floating point arithmetic. In any case the interior structure of a subroutine will depend upon its location in the memory. For example, the lefthand address of the second word in the square root routine (Library Code R1) refers to the eighth word of the routine. If the routine begins at location 10, this address must be 18. But if the routine begins at location 97, this address must be 105. The use of subroutines is very awkward unless problems of address changing can be easily handled.

Another principal nuisance in coding is the number system
used by the Illiac. In the sexadecimal system using Illiac notation
(see Chapter 2), the 1024 addresses of the memory are represented
by numbers between 0 and 3LL. It is much more convenient if addresses
can be expressed in decimal form with the Illiac doing the necessary
converting to the binary system.

With the Decimal Order Input every number corresponding
to the address part of an order must be written in the decimal system. These decimal numbers are always converted to sexadecimal
(i.e., binary) form by the Decimal Order Input.

The Decimal Order Input overcomes the obstacles of changing addresses in subroutines and of converting from decimal to
binary form. It also provides certain other useful service.

5.1 RELATIVE AND FIXED ADDRESSES. If we can devise
some way of using addresses in decimal form, we never need the 6
characters K, S, N, J, F, L in an address and can use them for other
purposes. Let us consider a program beginning in location 11 of
the memory, as shown in Table 5.1.

11	40	1
	S5	1
12	L4	13
	46	20
13	51	1
	10	1

Table 5.1

Program Beginning at Location 11

5-2

The same program, if begun at location 20, would read as in Table 5.2.

20	40	1
	S5	1
21	L4	22
	46	29
22	51	1
	10	1

Table 5.2
Program Beginning at Location 20

The second word has changed. But if we mark each address which depends upon the location of the routine with the symbol L and each address which is independent of the location of the routine with the symbol F, we have the program in Table 5.3.

0	40	1F
	S5	1F
1	L4	2L
	46	9L
2	51	1F
	10	1F

Table 5.3
Program With Relative and Fixed Addresses

The addresses ending in L are <u>relative to the location of the first word of the routine.</u>

5-3

We can now write each subroutine as if it begins at location zero provided we add to each L-terminated address the location of the first word of the routine when we store the routine. We shall do this by introducing a new symbol K.

5.2 **DIRECTIVES.** Orders which are written for the Illiac use two sexadecimal function digits followed by an address. We follow this convention even in the case of pseudo orders. A <u>directive</u> is such a pseudo order. When we want a group of orders to be placed in memory locations n, n+1, n+2, . . ., we punch on the tape the directive

$$00 \quad nK \ ^{1)}.$$

The Decimal Order Input will recognize this as a directive and will place the orders following the directive in pairs in the locations n, n+1, n+2, . . ., starting with the left hand side of location n. It will add n to the address of any order terminated with L before placing it in position. The directive 00 nK is not placed in the memory. Thus if we have 00 11K followed by the orders of Table 5.3 we will place in the memory the code given in Table 5.1, while the code of Table 5.2 would be obtained by using the directive 00 20K.

5.3 ASSEMBLING OF ORDERS. Since each address ends with an alphabet character and since there are always two function digits, the Decimal Order Input can distinguish between address digits and function digits. The Decimal Order Input uses the fixed storage

---

[1] We shall use small letters to represent decimal quantities and capital letters to represent sexadecimal quantities.

locations 0, 1, and 2 as temporary storage. After two function digits
have been read and shifted to a right-hand order position in location 1 the routine converts the decimal address n to binary form
$n \times 2^{-39}$ and <u>adds</u> it to the function digits. The order pair in location 1 is then stored. Next the contents of 1 are shifted left 20
places and the next order is formed as before. Again the order
pair in location 1 is stored in the same address as the previous
time, but now the <u>correctly assembled</u> order pair has been stored.
The address of the store order which is assembling the program is
increased <u>every other time.</u> Thus the left-hand 20 digits of
location 1 always contain the previous order while the next 8
digits of location 1 contain the function digits of the order being
put in.

When the address ends in K (a directive) it is stored in
location 2 and is added to each L terminated address in location 1
before the appropriate order is stored.

5.4 <u>DECIMAL ADDRESSES.</u> The address is converted one
digit at a time as it is read from the tape. This kind of conversion makes it unnecessary to write non-significant zeros, so
orders may have the form L5 7L, 40 1021F, 26 L, etc. Indeed,
we are not restricted to addresses smaller than 1024 and may use
anything we please. If the address exceeds 4095 it will add to
the function digits (remember that there are two unused digits
between the function digits and the address), but even this may
be made use of as we shall see below in Section 5.6.

5-5

5.5 STARTING THE PROGRAM. After the Decimal Order Input has placed a program in the memory we must start the program. This is done by using the terminating symbol N. The symbol N causes the order which it follows to be obeyed. It is used with a control transfer order which must appear on the tape as if it were a left-hand order. It will never be stored in the memory, other than as the right-hand order in location 1.

For example, the order 26 pN will be obeyed and will transfer control to the left-hand order at address p. Any unconditional transfer order may be used. The order 20 qN will stop the computer, and when the computer is started again control will go to the right-hand order at address q. The addresses p and q are fixed addresses.

Control can also be transferred using a relative address, for the previous order with its adjusted address is always in the left-hand side of location 1. Therefore the two orders 22 rL 26 1N will cause control to be transferred to address r relative to the last directive if 22 rL is the right-hand order of the last order pair, i.e., if the phase is correct.

5.6 INPUT OF DECIMAL FRACTIONS. In section 5.4 it was pointed out that an address is formed and added to the function digits. This address could be as large as $2^{39} - 1$ without getting into the sign digit, and any positive integer n could be input as $n \times 2^{-39}$ by letting the left-hand order and the right-hand function digits be zero. For example, the "order pair" 00F 002896F would appear as 2896×2^{-39}. Hence a 12 digit right-hand address smaller

5-6

than 2^{39} (about 5.5×10^{11}) could then be converted to a decimal fraction by multiplying it by $2^{39}/10^{12}$.

This is done when the terminating symbol J is used. For example, the characters OOF 002969 0000 0000J would cause the quantity 0.296 to be placed in the memory. Zeros at the end cannot be omitted, but preceding zeros can be omitted. Do not omit function digits. Remember that this is essentially an integer input. The range can be extended by using the left-hand function digits, for they are simply a number to which the right-hand address is added after being multiplied by $2^{39}/10^{12}$. The left-hand function digits 40, 80, NO represent 1/2, -1, -1/2. Thus numbers could be input as follows:

-0.8888 8888 8888 as 80F 00 1111 1111 1112J,

0.7854 3216 0000 as 40F 00 2854 3216 0000J.

This is not an efficient way to read decimal fractions into the machine, but it is convenient for occasional numbers scattered through the program.

5.7 PRE-SET PARAMETERS. MODIFICATION OF ORDERS. The remaining unused alphabetic sexadecimal character is S. This is used to modify orders by using pre-set parameters. The symbol S differs from the other terminating symbols in that it is always followed by another single character which may be any of the 13 sexadecimal characters 3 to L. The termination SD on an address causes the content of location D = 3, 4, . . . ,.F, L, to be added to the order while it is in a right-hand position as

5-7

described in Section 5.3 and before it is placed in the memory.
This is for either right or left-hand orders of completely assembled
order pairs. For example, if location J contains 7×2^{-39}, the
order pair L5 20SJ 40 30SJ will be modified to read L5 27F 40
37F before being stored. This facility is very convenient for
using parameters with a program because the program can be written
with orders of the form L5 S3, L4 S4, and if locations 3 and 4
have been previously set the parameters will be added appropriately
as the program is read into the machine.

Many examples of pre-set parameters can be found in the
library. In Illinois Code P6, Single Column Print, the parameter
00F 00mF is used to specify the printing of m decimal digits and
must be placed in location 3 before Code P6 is read. Thus if we
wish to place Code P6 in locations beginning with 50 and to print
7 decimal places, the pertinent part of the program tape would
read

00	3K	Directive
00	F	Place 7×2^{-39} in
00	7F	location 3
00	50K	Directive
Code P6		Place Code P6 beginning with location 50.

5.8 EXAMPLE OF USE OF DECIMAL ORDER INPUT. The decimal Order Input has 25 words and occupies locations 999 to 1023
in the memory. It is placed in these locations with its own bootstrap input which then transfers control to the Decimal Order Input

so that it can take over the control of program input. Let us consider the following simple example:

> Compute to 10 decimal places the square roots of
> $\pi/10$ and $e/10$ using the Square Root Routine (Code
> R1 and the Single Column Print routine (Code P6).
> We have the following data:
>
> (a) Code R1 - 9 words, closed, finds
>   square root of argument placed in
>   A and places answer in A.
>
> (b) Code P6 - 14 words, closed, prints
>   words in A to m decimal places followed
>   by carriage return and line-feed. Con-
>   tents of address 3 must contain m x 2^{-39}
>   as Code P6 is input.

In this program, the code for which is given in Table
5.4 on the following page, we have scattered the orders through
the memory to indicate how directives are used. Notice that the
arrangement on the tape is arbitrary after the Decimal Order Input
except that the parameter in address 3 must be in place when Code
P6 is being input. The parameter is used in word 6 of Code P6,
this word being

> 19 63S3
> 50   F

Thus the address of the 19 order was set to 9 (73 = 9 mod 64) for
counting the number of digits to be printed.

Notice also that the directive 00 560K can be changed

MEMORY LOCATION	PROGRAM TAPE	REMARKS
999 - 1023	Decimal Order Input	Routine X1
	00 10K	Directive
10 - 18	Square Root Routine	Routine R1
	00 3K	Directive
3	00 F	Parameter
	00 10F	
	00 30K	Directive
30 - 43	Print Routine	Routine P6
	00 50K	Directive
50	00 F	$\pi/10$
	00 314159265359J	
51	00 F	$e/10$
	00 271828182846J	
	00 560K	Directive
560	L5 50F	$\pi/10$ to A
	50 L	Link
561	26 10F	To Routine R1
	50 1L	Link
562	26 30F	To Routine P6
	L5 51F	$e/10$ to A
563	22 3L	Waste Order
	50 3L	Link
564	26 10F	To Routine R1
	50 4L	Link
565	26 30F	To Routine P6
	OF F	Stop
566	22 6L	Waste
	26 L	Start Program at
	24 1N	relative location 0 after stop

Table 5.4

Use of Decimal Order Input

so that the words following it are placed differently but that no other change need be made to move these words because the program was started using a relative address. The waste order at location 566 is required so that 24 1N will have a left-hand location.

5.9 <u>USE WITH INTERLUDES.</u> <u>RETAINED DIRECTIVE.</u> An interlude is a computation performed during the input of a program, the input being interrupted and then resumed.

A tape bearing a library routine may begin with an interlude which is placed in locations destined eventually to hold the routine itself. When the words of the interlude have been read control is directed to it, the interlude is executed, and then input is resumed. The next part of the tape carries the routine itself which is written over the interlude. The purpose of the interlude is usually to prepare some orders or constants required for the routine. For example, a printing routine, where the number of digits printed is determined by a preset parameter, may use an interlude to compute the roundoff constant.

Input is resumed after the interlude by transferring control to the left side of location 999 (3F7 sexadecimal). Either the first word on the tape must contain the needed directive 00 mK or Q must contain $m \times 2^{-39}$.

If, upon resuming input, it is desired to retain the <u>last used directive,</u> control should be transferred to the right side of 1014 with $m \times 2^{-39}$ in A. The next words on the tape will be placed in m, m+1, . . . , retaining the previous relative address. <u>The</u>

5-11

interlude must not use location 2.

  5.10 <u>STOPPING THE TAPE.</u> The order 20 1019N on the
tape will stop the computer and will have no other effect. Upon
being started the tape will continue being read from where it stopped.

  5.11 <u>PLACING THE DECIMAL ORDER INPUT. BOOTSTRAPS.</u>
Up to this point we have not said how the Decimal Order Input is
itself put into the Illiac. It occupies locations 999 to 1023,
the last 25 positions of the electrostatic memory, and it is placed
in the memory with a bootstrap input routine.

  With panel switches we can clear the control counter to
zero and place the order pair 80 40F 40 F in the order register.
The code in Table 5.4, which must be written with sexadecimal
addresses, will then place the Decimal Order Input in the memory.

800028
40 001

80 028
40 002

19 026
26 000

80 028
40(000) 2)

L4 001
40 001

80 028
40(3F6)

Table 5.4

Tape for Bootstrap Input Routine

---

2 Parentheses are often placed around addresses which change during
the course of a program.

This bootstrap actually places the 3-word routine (shown in both
sexadecimal and decimal forms) of Table 5.5 in the memory and starts
it

	L4	001		L4	1F
0	40	001	0	40	1F
	80	028		80	40F
1	40	(3F7)	1	40	(999)F
	19	026		19	38F
2	26	000	2	26	F

Table 5.5

Memory Contents for Bootstrap Input Routine

at location 1. Clearly it will take the next words on the tape
and start putting them at location 999F. To stop the input we
place the order pair 22 3LS 00 001 (That is 22 1019F 00 1F)
on the tape so that it gets put into location 0. The control
will be transferred to the right-hand side of location 1019F and
the Decimal Order Input will be started.

This bootstrap input may be used with any code and it
or something like it must be used to input programs whenever the
Decimal Order Input has been overwritten.

The term bootstrap start is often used for tapes which

are started by setting the order register to 80 40F 40 F and
the control counter to zero.

CHAPTER 6

SCALING

With the convention adopted for the Illiac (See Chapter 2), only numbers which lie in the range $-1 \leq x < 1$ can be held in the registers. Since most problems require numbers outside this range, some scaling process is usually needed to fit a problem to the machine. It is necessary that <u>each</u> <u>number</u> at <u>every</u> <u>stage</u> of a calculation lie within the capacity of the machine. The organization required to assure this is sometimes trivial, but in many instances it is the very essence of the problem.

6.1 <u>SCALING</u> <u>BY</u> <u>SHIFTING</u>. Although the number 2 lies outside the range of Illiac numbers, we can multiply and divide numbers by powers of 2 by shifting. Thus the left shift order 00 5F will cause AQ to be multiplied by $2^{10} = 1024$. Similarly, the right shift order 10 9F will divide AQ by $2^9 = 512$. A knowledge of the use of the shift orders is essential to an understanding of scaling.

6.2 <u>NUMBERS</u> <u>WITH</u> <u>THE</u> <u>BINARY</u> <u>POINT</u> <u>SHIFTED</u>. Let us consider the problem of computing with numbers in which the binary point has been moved 10 places to the right of its Illiac position. We are then dealing with numbers in the range $-1024 \leq y \leq 1024 - 2^{-29}$. Let these numbers be designated by N_{10}. Then we have $N_{10}(m) = 2^{10} N(m)$.

We can formulate rules for doing arithmetic with the numbers N_{10}. Addition and subtraction are simple. If $N(q) = N(m) + N(n)$, then

$$2^{10} \, N(q) = 2^{10} \, N(m) + 2^{10} \, N(n)$$

and

$$N_{10}(q) = N_{10}(m) + N_{10}(n).$$

Thus the Illiac addition rules hold.

Multiplication requires a shift to the left of 10 places. We want

$$N_{10}(q) = N_{10}(m) \times N_{10}(n).$$

Thus we require

$$2^{10} \, N(q) = 2^{10} \, N(m) \times 2^{10} \, N(n)$$

and

$$N(q) = 2^{10} \, N(m) \times N(n).$$

We may consider several simple routines to carry out the multiplication. The method given by (b) is probably the best.

(a)   The shortest method merely multiplies and shifts. Notice that a 75 order must be used rather than a 74 order because the least significant digit of $N_{10}(p)$ is now 2^{-29} and not 2^{-39}. A bias of -2^{-30} is introduced by the absence of a roundoff. The program is given in Table 6.1.

(b)   This method rounds off by adding 2^{-30} to $N_{10}(p)$, giving an unbiased result. The program is given in Table 6.2.

6-2

50 mF	N(m) to Q	
75 nF	N(m) x N(n) to AQ	
00 10F	2^{10} N(m) x N(n)	
40 pF	to p.	

Table 6.1

Multiplication with Binary Point Shifted

19 10F	2^{-11} to A
50 nF	N(m) to Q
74 nF	N(m) x N(n) + 2^{-50} to AQ
00 10F	2^{10} N(m) x N(n) + 2^{-40} to A
40 pF	to p.

Table 6.2

Unbiased Multiplication with
Binary Point Shifted

(c)   A roundoff similar to that of division is obtained
with the program given in Table 6.3.

t	50 mF	N(m) to Q
	75 nF	N(m) x N(n) to AQ
	00 9F	2^{9} N(m) x N(n) to AQ
	50 tF	2^{-1} Q = 1
	00 1F	This makes 2^{-39} A = 1;
		N(A) = 2^{10} N(m) x N(n)
	40 qF	to q.

Table 6.3

Division-Type Roundoff in Multiplication
with Binary Point Shifted

In Table 6.3 the order 50 tF is used simply because the word at location t has a 1 in the proper place.

In division we also need an extra shift to restore the quotient to the proper range. But here the shift precedes the divide order and no special arrangements for roundoff are necessary. We want

$$N_{10}(q) = N_{10}(m)/N_{10}(n).$$

Hence

$$2^{10}N(q) = N(m)/N(n),$$

and

$$N(q) = 2^{-10} N(m)/N(n).$$

The following program in Table 6.4 will carry out the required operations:

L5	mF	$N(m)$ to A
10	10F	$2^{-10} N(m)$
66	nF	$2^{-10} N(m)/N(n)$
S5	F	to A
40	qF	to q.

Table 6.4

Division with Binary Point Shifted

It can be noted that by using such relations as

$$10^{p} = 2^{n} x \quad \frac{10^{p}}{2^{n}}$$

6-4

where $10^p < 2^n$ we can use decimal scaling although it will be slower and clumsier to handle because of the factors $10^p/2^n$.

    6.3 <u>SCALING A FULL PROBLEM</u>. There are conceptually two ways in which we can approach the scaling of a problem; both give the same program.

> (a) We can alter the problem using such substitutions as $x^1 = 100x$ or $p^1 = 32p$, so that the modified problem has all its variables less than one but retaining full significance.

> (b) We can use scaled numbers inside the machine to represent the variables. That is, we can use $x/100$ instead of x and $p/32$ instead of p.

The final result must be such that the variables lie within machine range and retain sufficient accuracy. Constants greater than one can be represented by numbers less than one in conjunction with scaling factors. For example, multiplication by 5.63 can be done by multiplying by $5.63/8$ and shifting left 3 places.

    Let us consider the following simple problem:

    <u>Example 1.</u> Program the Illiac to compute the quantities

$$y = \frac{e^x}{1 + x^2}$$

at intervals of 0.01 from $x = 0$ to $x = 6$.

    We note that we must scale x. Since the largest value of

x is 6, let us use x/8 inside the computer because this will minimize the loss of significant figures.

What scaling factor is needed for y? A rough estimate shows that y does not exceed $e^6/(1 + 36) \sim 11$, so that we shall compute and store y/16.

Library Routine S2, the exponential routine, will give valid results only if x is negative. We therefore write

$$e^{x/8} = e \times e^{-1 + x/8}$$

so that
$$e^x = (e^{x/8})^8.$$

Now $y/16 = \dfrac{e^x}{16 \times 64} \times \dfrac{1}{1/64 + x^2/64},$

and $\dfrac{e^x}{16 \times 64} = \left\{ \left[(e^{-1 + x/8} \times e/4)^2 \times 2 \right]^2 \times 2 \right\}^2.$

We shall store the constants e/4 and 1/16. Each part of the computation is within machine capacity. We proceed as follows:

  (a) Square x/8 and add 1/64,

  (b) Call the result R and store it,

  (c) Evaluate $e^{-1 + x/8}$ with Library Routine S2,

  (d) Multiply by e/4 and square,

  (e) Double and square,

(f)   Double and square again. Call the result P.

(g)   Form y/16 by dividing P by R.

Accuracy in the Result.   Let us now consider how much accuracy we obtain. If x/8 is near unity, numbers remain large during the calculation and we do not lose significance by subtracting nearly equal numbers or by other ill-conditioning.

However, when x/8 is small we notice that we form $e^x/(16 \times 64)$ quite accurately and then divide by R $\sim$ 1/64 which is about equivalent to a left shift of 6 places and loses 6 binary digits on the right. We can prevent this if we perform the division while the double-length P is in AQ.

Accuracy in the Argument.   We should also consider the accuracy of the argument x/8. It can be formed either by successively adding the increment 0.01/8 = 0.00125 or by counting and multiplying. The adding method is not so good because the quantity 0.00125 will not be stored exactly and the accumulated roundoff error obtained by the time x is 6 (which requires 600 additions) may be troublesome.

The counting method avoids this trouble. Any x/8 is n × 0.01/8. Hence we have

$$x/8 = n \times 0.01/8$$

$$= (n \times 2^{-39}) \times 0.64 \times 2^{30}$$

If we store 0.64 and count to get $n \times 2^{-39}$, we can use the following set of orders to get $x/8$ (where we have used arguments in place of addresses):

$$
\begin{array}{ll}
50 & n \times 2^{-39} \\
75 & 0.64 \\
00 & 30 \\
40 & x/8.
\end{array}
$$

The program for the entire calculation of $y/16$ is given in Table 6.5 on page 6-9 where we have again used arguments instead of addresses.

Example 2: Solve the pair of simultaneous equations

$$ax + by + c = 0$$
$$dx + ey + f = 0$$

where the coefficients are in absolute values less than $1/2$ and where the answers are known to lie within machine range. Retain as much accuracy as is reasonably possible.

We can distinguish two cases:

(a) If $|a| \geq |d|$, then

$$y = - \frac{dc/a - f}{bd/a - e} ,$$

$$x = - \frac{c + by}{a}$$

6-8

ORDER	ARGUMENT		ORDER	ARGUMENT
F5	$n \times 2^{-39}$		50	$e^{-1} + x/8$
40	$(n + 1) \times 2^{-39}$		7J	$ex2^{-2}$
50	$(n + 1) \times 2^{-39}$		40	$e^{x/8}/4$
75	.64		50	$e^{x/8}/4$
00	30		75	$e^{x/8}/4$
40	$x/8$		00	1
50	$x/8$		40	$e^{x/4}/8$
7J	$x/8$		50	$e^{x/4}/8$
L4	1/64		75	$e^{x/4}/8$
40	$1/64 + x^2/64$		00	1
L5	$x/8$		40	$e^{x/2}/32$
L4	-1		50	$e^{x/2}/32$
50			75	$e^{x/2}/32$
26	to S2		66	$1/64 + x^2/64$
40	$e^{-1} + x/8$		S5	
			40	$y/16$

Table 6.5

Calculation of $e^x/(1 + x^2)$

6-9

(b)   If $\left| \, d \, \right| > \left| \, a \, \right|$, then

$$y = - \frac{c - fa/d}{b - ae/d}$$

$$x = - \frac{f + ey}{d}$$

In this program we shall follow the conventions of the Decimal Order Input (See Chapter 5). Notice that divisions are always made using a full 78 digit dividend to retain as much accuracy as possible. The program treats the two cases (a) and (b) separately, distinguishing with the 36 order at 1L. Locations 0 and 1 in the memory are used as temporary storage. The program is given in Table 6.6 on pages 6-12 and 6-13.

6.4   ADJUSTABLE SCALING FACTORS.   It is not always possible to arrange a program so that a single scaling factor can be used throughout the calculation. Then it is necessary to make tests at appropriate places to discover when variables are becoming too large or too small and to make proper adjustments in the scaling factors. For many problems it is advantageous to have the variable less than 1/2. Then two numbers can be added or multiplied without exceeding capacity. By using the LL n order we place $1/2 + \left| N(n) \right|$ in A. Hence A is positive if $\left| N(n) \right| < 1/2$ and A is negative if $\left| N(n) \right| \geq 1/2$.

6.5   CONTINUOUS SCALING.   FLOATING POINT ROUTINES.   For calculations in which continual tests are required to maintain accuracy floating point routines (See also Section 4.7) may be used. These

routines represent numbers as $y = a \times 10^b$ and store a and b. Thus
they can represent accurately the numbers in some large range such
as, for example, $10^{-63} \leq y < 10^{63}$ where y has 30 significant binary
digits. There are two such routines in the Illinois Program Library.
The first, Library Routine A1 is as described above. The second,
Library Routine A4 is a multiple precision floating point program
in which numbers lies in the range $10^{-153} < y < 10^{153}$ with y
having 20 significant decimal places.

Floating point routines are slow because numbers are
scaled at each step of the calculation. Certain conveniences have
been programmed in, however, and these to some extent compensate for
the extra time required and also simplify the programming.

0	L7 22L	$\left	a \right	- \left	d \right	$
	L2 25L	
1	36 13L	$\left	a \right	< \left	d \right	$; f to Q
	50 27L	
2	75 22L	fa/d
	66 25L	
3	S1 F	
	L4 24L	
4	40 F	-fa/d + c to 0
	50 22L	
5	75 26L	ae/d
	66 25L	
6	S1 F	
	L4 23L	
7	40 1F	-ae/d + b to 1
	L5 F	
8	66 1F	$(-fa/d + c)/(-ae/d + b) = -y$
	S1 F	
9	40 29L	y to 29L
	50 29L	
10	75 26L	
	L4 27L	(ey + f)
11	66 25L	
	S1 F	$-(ey + f)/d = x$
12	40 28L	x to 28L
	0F F	STOP
13	50 23L	$\left	a \right	\geq \left	d \right	$; b to Q
	75 25L	
14	66 22L	bd/a
	S5 F	

Table 6.6

Solution of Two Simultaneous Equations

15	LO	26L	
	40	F	bd/a - e to 0
16	50	25L	d to Q
	75	24L	
17	66	22L	dc/a
	S1	F	
18	L4	27L	
	66	F	$(-dc/a + f)/(bd/a - e) = y$
19	S5	F	
	40	29L	y to 29L
20	75	23L	by
	L4	24L	
21	66	22L	$(by + c)/a = -x$
	22	11L	Control to 11L
22			a
23			b
24			c
25			d
26			e
27			f
28			x
29			y

Table 6.6 (Continued)

Solution of Two Simultaneous Equations

.

CHAPTER 7

MACHINE METHODS AND CODING TRICKS

There are usually a number of special techniques which
can be used on any particular digital computer and which will simplify programming. Some of these techniques are applicable on many
different computers but usually, as is the case in those which follow,
they result from particular orders or combinations of orders which
are peculiar to an individual machine. This chapter is concerned
with a number of unrelated sections having to do with operations
which frequently arise in programming.

7.1 THE SUMMATION OF PRODUCTS. We often need to form
sums of products, and on the Illiac this cannot be directly done in
the accumulator. The accuracy can often be enhanced by performing
a summation either exactly or with only one round-off error. This
is comparatively easy to do using the 74 order. All that we need
·to do is to place the least significant half of the partially summed
products into the accumulator before performing the 74 order. In
fact, this can usually be done by an S5 order because the quotient
register will usually hold the last single half of a summed product.
Then, since 74 n gives $N(n) Q + 2^{-39}A$, we obtain the double-length
product in AQ. Of course, the most significant part of the previously summed products needs to be added using an L4 order.

Using similar schemes we can also arrange to add or
subtract products with double-length accuracy in a program. As a

7-1

first example we shall sum 50 double-length products, assuming we
do not exceed capacity.

Example 1: Place the rounded sum

$$\sum_{i=0}^{49} N(100 + i)\, N(150 + i)$$

in location 0.   The program is given in Table 7.1

m	41	F	Clear location 0 for sum.
	26	1L	Wasted order.
m+1	50	8L	Put 1/2 in Q.
	L5	11L	Set i = 0.
m+2	40	3L	
	S5	F	Round off (See Section 7.2).
m+3	50	( )F	
	74	( )F	N(100 + i)×N(150 + i)
m+4	L4	F	
	40	F	
m+5	L5	9L	Increase i by 1.
	L4	3L	
m+6	40	3L	
	L0	10L	Test for i ≥ 150
m+7	32	2L	Re-enter loop.
	0F	F	Stop.
m+8	40	F	Roundoff constant = 1/2
	00	F	
m+9	00	1F	Increment
	00	1F	
m+10	J0	150F	End constant
	74	200F	
m+11	50	100F	Starting constant
	74	150F	

Table 7.1
Program for Example 1

7.2   <u>REVERSING THE CONTROL TRANSFER. FURTHER DISCUSSION OF

<u>EXAMPLE 1.</u>   There is a second coding trick in Example 1. The end

constant, instead of being 50 150F   74 200F has had -1 added to it,

making the first order JO 150F. The effect is to reverse the sense

of the following 32 order (in location m + 7) so that we transfer

control to re-enter the repetitive loop. If this had not been done

a 22 order following the 32 order would have been required and the

32 would have transferred to OFF. Thus a half word was saved. This

technique is equivalent to having a conditional transfer order act

when the accumulator is negative.

Another coding trick might have been used to save a full

word. The left-hand order at m + 1 puts 1/2 in Q so that it may be

used to round off on the first step of the sum, this being the sole

roundoff. Instead of storing 1/2 in m + 8 we could have used the

order pair in m + 2 as the roundoff constant. This order pair is

1/2 plus at most 2^{-9} and would serve quite well.

As a second example we consider a summation of two products

with a single roundoff.

Example 2:   Given

cos θ in 10,

sin θ in 11,

x   in 12,

y   in 13,

place the rounded quantity (x cos θ + y sin θ) in

location 20 and the rounded quantity (-x sin θ + y cos θ)

in location 21. The program is given in Table 7.2.

7-3

m	50	10F	$x \cos \theta + 2^{-40}$
	7J	12F	
m+1	40	F	Most significant half to location 0
	S5	F	Least significant half to A
m+2	50	11F	$y \sin \theta + 2^{-39}$ (l.s. half of $x \cos \theta + 2^{-40}$)
	74	13F	
m+3	L4	F	Add most significant half of $x \cos \theta + 2^{-40}$
	40	20F	Store $x \cos \theta + y \sin \theta + 2^{-40}$
m+4	50	11F	$-x \sin \theta + 2^{-40}$
	79	12F	
m+5	40	F	
	S5	F	
m+6	50	10F	$y \cos \theta + 2^{-39}$ (l.s. half of $-x \cos \theta + 2^{-40}$)
	74	13F	
m+7	L4	F	
	40	21F	Store $-x \sin \theta + y \cos \theta + 2^{-40}$

Table 7.2

Program for Example 2.

7.3 <u>BINARY SWITCHES.</u> It is sometimes necessary to do two different operations alternately. This can be done by changing the sign of a number each time we pass it so that it will be alternately positive and negative. Usually it is not necessary to use a special number for this because some number or order pair in the rest of the program may be used. To accomplish the switch an L1 order followed by a 40 order is used to change the sign of the number and put it back in its location with sign changed. A conditional transfer order may then be used to decide which of two sequences will be performed.

A variation is the requirement that an order (or order pair) take on two different values alternately. This can be accomplished by using the identities

$$b = (b + a) - a,$$
$$\text{and} \quad a = (b + a) - b.$$

Thus if the current value of an order (or order pair) is subtracted from the sum the other value is obtained.

Example 3: Arrange a program to alter the address of the left-hand order at (m+2) so that it takes on the values 0 and 5 alternately. A program for this is given in Table 7.3

m	any order		
	L5	pF	Put sum of orders in A
m+1	L0	2L	Form alternate address
	40	2L	Store alternate address at (m+2)
m+2	L5	(0)F	
	L4	12F	Normal program order
p	FK	5F	Sum of L5 0F L4 12F
	F8	24F	and L5 5F L4 12F

Table 7.3
Binary Switch

In Table 7.3 only a single address is taking on alternate values and it is also possible to carry out the switch using the program of Table 7.4. In Table 7.4 the 50 5F order at location m is provided for the switch. If some order which needed address 5F could be used here, we should be very well-off indeed.

7-5

```
m        50  5F
         L5  mF

m+1      LO  (m+2)F
         46  (m+2)F

m+2      L5  (0)F
         L4  (12)F
```

Table 7.4

Binary Switch

7.4   TESTS FOR 0 AND -1.   In order to test for a particular number value held inside the machine it is generally necessary
to use two tests. However, the numbers 0 and -1 can be tested for
using absolute value orders and a single test. In machine language
0 is the only number whose negative absolute value is positive, and
-1 is the only number whose positive absolute value is negative.
Thus we can test for 0 using an L3 order followed by a conditional
transfer order, and we can test for -1 using an L7 order. Similarly,
we can test for -2^{-39} and $1 - 2^{-39}$ by using F3 and F7 orders, respectively.

    Example 4:   Transfer control to location 200 if A
    is zero but transfer control to location 300 if A
    is non-zero. Two ways to do this are given in Tables
    7.5 and 7.6. The program of Table 7.5 has only two
    words. The program of Table 7.6 has four words but
    will be faster than the other if A is usually negative.

7-6

Moreover, the program of Table 7.6 can be used
to transfer control to any of three locations depending upon whether A is positive, negative or zero.

m	40	F	A to 0
	L3	F	$- \left| N(0) \right|$ to A
m+1	36	200F	To 200 if A $\,$ 0, i.e., if A = 0
	26	300F	To 300 if A $\neq$ 0

Table 7.5

Testing for Zero

m	36	1L	
	26	300F	To 300 if A $\quad$ 0
m+1	LO	pF	A $- 2^{-39}$
	36	300F	To 300 if A $- 2^{-39}$ $\quad$ 0, i.e., if A $\quad$ 0
m+2	26	200F	To 200 otherwise, i.e., if A = 0
p	00	F	Constant 2^{-39}
	00	1F	

Table 7.6

Testing for Sign

7.5   <u>USE OF ORDERS AND ADDRESSES AS CONSTANTS.</u>   SV and
KV orders do not use their addresses, so these addresses can often
be used for other purporses. For instance, they may be used to store
a starting address taken by a cycling order or an increment which
is used to change an address. In such cases we naturally use 42 or
46 orders to make certain that the function digits do not become
altered.

In the following example the address of a K5 order is used as a counter.

Example 5:   Given the positive number a in A, write a closed subroutine which will furnish the positive integer m such that $1/2 \leq 2^m a < 1$. The program is given in Table 7.7

m	40	F	Store a at location 0
	K5	F	Form link
m+1	42	4L	Plant link
	43	L	Clear counter
m+2	L5	F	
	00	1F	Shift a
m+3	40	F	
	36	5L	Test to see if $2^p a$ 1
m+4	L4	L	Counter to A
	22	( )F	Link
m+5	F5	L	Count
	40	L	
m+6	26	2L	Re-enter loop
	00	F	Waste order

Table 7.7
Address Use in K5 Order

7.6   RESETTING AND STARTING OF CYCLES OF ORDERS.   In many cases we have cycles of orders, some of which are being modified by the same increment. In such cases the variable addresses can all

7-8

be modified by modifying one order and then deriving the other orders
(or addresses) by adding the constant difference between the variable
orders. When this is done it is economical to use the same orders
to set these addresses when the cycle is begun. The following example with the program given in Table 7.8 illustrates this:

Example 6: For i = 0, 1, . . . , 99 place   in
location 200 + i the sum N(10) + N(100 + i) + N(200 + i).

m	L5	7L	
	26·	4L	Set i = 0
m+1	L5	10F	Form N(10) + N(100 + i) + N(200 + i)
	L4	F	and put in 200 + i
m+2	L4	F	
	40	F	
m+3	L5	7L	
	L4	2L	Increase i in m + 2
m+4	40	2L	Increase i in m + 1 and test for end
	L0	9L	
m+5	42	1L	
	36	1L	
m+6	0F	F	Stop
	00	F	Waste order
m+7	L4	200F	Starting constant
	40	200F	
m+8	00	1F	Increment
	00	1F	
m+9	74	300F	End constant
	00	100F	Constant to change i in 2L

Table 7.8
Resetting of Addresses

In Example 6 the addresses in location m + 2 have been
changed and then that in m + 1 has been obtained from one of them.
Notice that the end test has been combined with the second address
change and that the end test constant is not L4 but 74 so that the
36 order at location m + 5 will cause re-entry to the repetitive loop.

When two orders have to be varied in a single cycle, it is
advantageous to let these form a single order pair as in Example 6
so that they can both be modified simultaneously by the same orders.
This arrangement is not always possible and the second best arrangement is to place the variable orders on the same side of their res-
pective order pairs so that the orders required to modify them will
be as simple as possible.

For very simple operations it is sometimes advantageous to
do three or four operations in a single cycle. This saves time
although the advantage is bought at the expense of more orders. This
is illustrated in Example 7.

Example 7: Add the numbers in memory locations
10 and 14, putting the sum in location 15. It is
simpler and faster, both in coding and in machine
operation, to use the program given at the top of
page 7-11 than to write a repetitive code which counts.

```
L5   10F
L4   11F
L4   12F
L4   13F
L4   14F
40   15F
```

7.7   USE OF THE QUOTIENT REGISTER FOR INTERCHANGES.   In
many programs we wish to replace the number in a certain storage
location and yet use the value that is there to continue with the calculation.   In such cases the old value can be placed in the quotient
register before the new value replaces it in the memory.   Thus, the
old value is available in the quotient register for further computation.

Example 8:   Store A in location 10, but use the old
N(10) as a dividend to form N(10)/N(11).   The program
is then

```
50   10F
40   10F

S5   F
66   11F
```

7.8   TESTING IF NUMBERS ARE GREATER THAN ONE-HALF.   When
scaling numbers it is very often necessary to test when numbers are
larger in magnitude than one-half.   This can easily be done with the
appropriate L or S order.   For example, the order LL n will cause the

accumulator to be negative if the magnitude of N(n) is greater than or equal to 1/2.

Example 9:   If $\left|N(10)\right| \geqq 1/2$ replace it by half its value. The program is given in Table 7.9.

m	LL	10F		$1/2 + \left|N(10)\right|$ to A
	32	(m+2)F		
m+1	L5	10F		
	10	1F		
m+2	40	10F		

Table 7.9
Scaling by Testing for One-half

7.9   <u>CONVERGENCE CRITERIA.</u>   When iterations or repetitive calculations are carried out we frequently want to stop when we have achieved the maximum accuracy. In some cases it is difficult to specify in advance the tolerances which can be used as end criteria because we have to compromise between achieving the greatest accuracy and yet assuring that we terminate the processes (i.e., don't loop).

In such cases it is worthwhile to use more complicated criteria which will give us maximum accuracy but which will not loop. One such criterion is to terminate the process if $e_n \geq e_{n+1}$ where e_i is some positive number which tends to zero as the process converges with increasing n. This criterion will terminate the process only when either e_i is the same for two successive iterations or when the roundoff error has actually caused it to increase.

7.10 <u>MARKING.</u> It is often possible to use marking techniques instead of the more usual counting processes. The simplest illustration of such a technique is Library Routine N3 where a sequence of numbers read from the tape is automatically terminated by the mark N. In this code instead of counting up to some predetermined number we test each character as it is read from the tape until it is N.

A binary digit is sometimes shifted as a marker; this is illustrated in the next example.

Example 10: Using a print routine stored at locations beginning with 50 print the 7 numbers in locations 10-16. The program is given in Table 7.10

0	19	7F	2^{-8} to 1F. This is the marker
	40	1F	
1	L5	1F	
	00	1F	Advance marker by shifting
2	40	1F	
	32	3L	Test for end
3	OF	F	Stop
	L5	1OF	
4	22	4L	Waste order
	50	4L	
5	26	50F	Enter print routine
	F5	3L	
6	40	3L	Increase address of number to be printed
	26	1L	Re-enter loop

Table 7.10

Use of a Marker

In the program of Table 7.10 the marker is shifted into the sign digit to indicate the end of the repetitive process.

This technique can be used in a similar way for completely internal programs. For example, when we are dealing with a group of numbers in the memory we may arrange that the storage location following the group contains some unique number such as 0 or -1. Then the code merely has to test for the presence of one of these numbers rather than for a predetermined count.

7.11 <u>REMAINDER IN INTEGER DIVISION.</u> In the general case it is difficult to compute the remainder from the residue that is left in the accumulator after a division. However, if we are dealing with positive integers less than 2^{+38} in magnitude we can do this quite readily. We place twice the dividend integer in the quotient register, clear the accumulator and divide by the divisor integer. The accumulator then contains twice the integer remainder and the quotient contains twice the integer. We store an integer m as m x 2^{-39}.

Example 11:   Divide the positive integer in location 20 by 10. Place the quotient in location 11 and the remainder in location 12. The program is given in Table 7.11.

m	51	20F	$m \times 2^{-39}$ to Q
	00	1F	$m \times 2^{-38}$ to AQ
m+1	66	4L	$(m \times 2^{-38})/(10 \times 2^{-39}) \times 2^{-1} = m/10$
	10	1F	
m+2	40	12F	Store remainder
	S5	F	
m+3	40	11F	Store quotient
	26	pF	
m·4	00	F	
	00	10F	

Table 7.11

Remainder in Integer Division

7.12   BINARY CHOPPING.   This is the method of repeated
subdivision of an interval. It is easy to code although it may be
wasteful of memory space and it is slow because it will usually take
the full 39 steps to go from an interval of length unity down to
one of length 2^{-39}.

If we use binary chopping to find the zero of a function,
we proceed as follows. We choose bounds for the zero, perhaps -1 as
a lower bound and +1 as an upper bound. Then we bisect the interval
and compute the function at the midpoint. Depending upon whether the
sign of the function at the midpoint agrees with the sign of the lower
or upper bound, we substitute the midpoint for the appropriate bound.
After 39 steps the difference between the two bounds will be 2^{-39}
and the zero will be determined.

The code will be simpler if the signs of the upper and lower bounds are known so that a comparison with the sign of the midpoint is not needed at each step. This is the case in Example 12.

Example 12:   Find the square root of a = 0.26943 by using a binary chopping technique on the function $a_n^2 - a$.

Here we choose initial upper and lower bounds of $1 - 2^{-39}$ and 0. Instead of counting 39 steps, a test has been included so that if $a_n^2 - a < 2^{-37}$ the code stops. The program is given in Table 7.12.

7.13   <u>EVALUATION OF POLYNOMIALS.</u>   Polynomials are best evaluated by use of a recurrence relation. Given the polynomial

$$f(x) = \sum_{i=0}^{n} a_i x^{n-i} = a_0 x^n + a_1 x^{n-1} + \ldots + a_{n-1} x + a_n,$$

we can express it in the form

$$S_{i+1} = x S_i + a_i,$$

$$S_0 = 0,$$

$$S_{n+1} = f(x).$$

0	L5	12L	
	10	1F	
1	40	F	$\bar{a}/2$ to location 0
	L5	13L	
2	10	1F	$(\bar{a} + \underline{a})/2 = a_n$ to 14L
	L4	F	
3	40	14L	
	50	14L	
4	7J	14L	
	LO	11L	
5	40	15L	$a_n^2 - a$ to 15L
	32	7L	
6	L5	14L	
	40	13L	Change $\underline{a}$
7	22	8L	
	L5	14L	
8	40	12L	Change $\bar{a}$
	L7	15L	
9	LO	16L	Test for $a_n^2 - a < 2^{-37}$
	36	L	
10	OF	F	Stop
	00	F	
11	00	F	$a = 0.26943$
	00	269430000000J	
12	7L	4095F	$\bar{a} = 1 - 2^{-39}$
	LL	4095F	
13	00	F	$\underline{a} = 0$
	00	F	
14	00	F	a_n
	00	F	
15	00	F	$a_n^2 - a$
	00	F	
16	00	F	2^{-37}
	00	4F	

Table 7.12

Square Root by Binary Chopping

If, as is often the case, the coefficients a_i are the
quantities $N(m+i)$ the recurrence relation becomes

$$S_{i+1} = x \; S_i + N(m+i),$$

$$S_0 = 0,$$

$$S_{n+1} = f(x)$$

Example 13 shows how a polynomial may be evaluated. In practice
the summation of products should be done with a 74 order as in
Example 1, but we do not wish to obscure the general idea here.

Example 13:   Given x in location 49 and coefficients
in locations 50 through 67 evaluate the polynomial

$$\sum_{i=0}^{17} x^{17-i} N(50+i).$$

The program is given in Table 7.13.

7.14   SHIFTING A LEFT WITHOUT SHIFTING Q.   The contents
of A may be shifted to the left (doubled) by adding A to itself.
This is slower than using a shift order but it has the advantage
that the Q register is not altered (as it would be by a shift order).
The order pair 40 nF L4 Nf will shift the contents of A one
place to the left for each use.

p	41	F	$S_0 = 0$
	50	49F	x
p+1	7J	F	$x\,S_i + N(50 + i)$
	L4	50F	
p+2	40	F	
	F5	1L	Increase i
p+3	40	1L	
	LO	5L	Test for end
p+4	32	L	
	OF	F	
p+5	LJ	F	End test constant
	L4	68F	

Table 7.13

Evaluation of a Polynomial

CHAPTER 8

CHECKING METHODS

To obtain a correctly working program from a written one
the coder must find and remove all of the coding errors. To the
person unfamiliar with coding it might seem that a careful inspection
of a program before it is run on the Illiac would remove all of the
coding blunders but unfortunately this is not true. It is necessary
to check the program on the machine to remove the remaining blunders
from a code, and it is unusual to find all blunders in one run on
the machine. As a general rule it will be necessary to have several
checking runs on the machine before a code is correct.

The number of coding errors in a program depends upon a
number of factors, including complexity, length of untested program,
programmer, and the care with which the code was inspected. It is
possible to remove most coding blunders from a program by carefully
inspecting it and it is best to obtain a person other than the coder
to inspect the code. In many cases this cannot be done, and then the
code should be set aside for as long as possible before being inspected.
This to some extent prevents a grooved mind from missing the flaws in
the program, for the coder remembers the general nature of the program but not the details where most errors occur.

8.1 COMMON BLUNDERS.   A great many of the coding mistakes
made by programmers are familiar ones which are made over and over again.

The list given in Table 8.1 is one of common errors. It should be pointed out, however, that this list is not complete, and that programmers develop their own idiosyncrasies and should be on guard for their own pet blunders.

8.2   THE DISCOVERY OF ERRORS. Errors are found by running the program and comparing the actual performance with the designed performance. That is, to find an error it is necessary to obtain information about the way a program runs. It is almost useless to have a program run through a long calculation and then print out the result. If the result is wrong, no information is usually available to explain why. Therefore, when checking a program we have to print out more information about the intermediate results than is required in the actual running of the program. There are many ways in which this can be done and the remainder of this chapter describes some of them.

Because we have to compare the intermediate stages of the calculation with those estimated by other means, it behooves us to choose parameters and variables so that the initial calculation is as simple as possible. Further trials will probably have to be run with more complicated calculations and with values designed to test the special cases and boundary limitations. Simple blunders should be detected and removed before an attempt is made to look for more subtle errors. Localization of mysterious errors can be effected by continually printing more and more information from smaller and smaller parts of the program until the error is found.

1. L5 orders used instead of L4 orders.
2. S5 orders omitted after divisions.
3. Orders terminated by L instead of F and vice-versa.
4. The renumbering of a code not complete after a modification has been made.
5. Rounded multiplication used when dealing with integers.
6. Control transfers to the wrong address or wrong order of an order pair.
7. Accumulating storage registers not cleared before a cycle of orders is entered.
8. The end condition for a cycle of orders not correct.
9. Allowing the temporary storage of a subroutine to erase useful data.
10. Using a 46 order instead of a 42 order and vice-versa.
11. Omitting directives and starting orders on the program tape.
12. Incorrectly remembering the specifications of a subroutine.
13. Forgetting to reset addresses when coming back to a cycle of orders.
14. Making corrections incorrectly.
15. Using the same relative addresses on correction words although the preceding directive is different from that of the program.
16. Overlooking the digits shifted from the quotient register to the accumulator on a left shift.
17. Attempting to convert fractions greater than one-half by using the J terminating symbol.

Table 8.1

Typical Blunders

8.3 SOURCES OF INFORMATION.

The Punch. The punch is the most effective way by which data can be extracted from the Illiac. However, there are other ways to obtain information, particularly when a program does not run far enough to punch any data at all.

The Reader. If the input tape stops before the entire program has been read into the memory, then an examination of the characters punched on the tape just ahead of the place where it stopped will often provide an explanation.

The Order Register and Control Counter. If the program is read in correctly but comes to a sudden unexpected stop, then the order register R_3 will exhibit the order on which the program stopped while the control counter will contain a number one greater than the storage location from which the order pair came. With this information the programmer can often discover the cause of failure of his program.

If the Illiac loops, observation of the slave tube will give an indication of how extensive the loop is. Then, if the machine is stopped and the contents of the order register and the control counter noted, we usually have enough data to identify the loop in our program.

8.4 MODIFICATIONS TO PROGRAMS. Temporary modifications often need to be made to a program while it is being checked. These may be for the purpose of correcting the program, for temporarily arranging the punching of extra data, or for some other purpose. In

such cases it is undesirable to repunch the entire program tape. The
modification can be carried out by "overwriting" the original program,
that is by replacing some of the orders already placed in the memory
by other orders. To do this a short extra tape is punched with suitable directives and words so that, when it is read into the memory
by the Decimal Order Input, the appropriate words of the original
program are replaced by those on the tape. For example, 00 523K
L5 4F 40 2F will cause the word at 523 to be replaced by L5 4F 40 2F.

In order to be able to use this technique of modifying a
program we must:

(a)   Prevent the original program from being started
       before the modification is made.

(b)   Transfer control to the Decimal Order Input so
       that the modification tape can be read into the
       memory.

(c)   Start the program after the modification has been
       made.

This can be done efficiently if the original program ends
with a stop transfer of control to the Decimal Order Input followed
by a transfer of control to the program. An example might be 24 999N
26 93N if it were necessary to transfer control to location 93 to
start the program.

If we wish to modify the program before starting it, all
this is necessary is to place the modification tape in the reader
before moving the switch to START. This will cause the modification
tape to be read instead of the 26 93N. The modification tape will

8-5

naturally have to end with 26 93N in order to start the program.

If the original program ends with a stop transfer of control
to itself instead of to the Decimal Order Input a slightly more complicated modification tape is necessary. An example might be 24 93N.
Then the sexadecimal order pair 26 3F7 00 000 is punched at the
head of the modification tape. When this tape is placed in the reader
the machine is completely restarted by setting the order register to
82 40F 40 F and the control counter to zero without, however, clearing
the memory. This results in the first order pair on the tape (namely
26 3F7 00 000) being transferred to location zero and being obeyed,
so that control is transferred to 3F7 sexadecimal or 999 decimal (the
Decimal Order Input), and the rest of the tape is read in the usual
way. This is a bootstrap start. See Section 5.11.

Corrections. As each coding blunder is found, a modification tape should be repunched to include all of the corrections. It
is not worthwhile repunching the entire program tape until all or a
large number of coding errors have been found.

8.5   BLOCKING ORDERS.   This is the name given to control
transfer orders which are used to replace normal program orders, so
that some printing or checking can be done at the point of replacement. Before control is restored to the program the replaced order
of the program is executed and the contents of the arithmetic registers are restored. Thus the original program is unaffected, but
the extra orders that are obeyed can be utilized to do printing of

desired data.

An example may illustrate this: Let us suppose that

    (a) we have a program in which we wish to
print N(19) after the left-hand order of
the order pair 40 9F L5 29F at storage
location 100, has been obeyed,

    (b) we wish to preserve the quotient register
but not the temporary storage of the print
subroutine,

    (c) locations 800-804 are unused by the program,

    (d) the program print routine starts at 200,

    (e) the original program ends with 24 999N 26 nN.

We then prepare the following modification tape:

MODIFICATION TAPE		COMMENTS
00	100K	Directive
40	9F	Plants blocking order in program
26	800F	
00	800K	Directive
S5	F	
40	4L	Stores Q at 804F
L5	19F	Enters print subroutine
50	1L	
26	200F	
L5	29F	Does omitted order
50	4L	Restores Q
26	101F	Control back to program
26	nN	Starts program

8.6   TYPES OF CHECKING ROUTINES. There are several types
of checking routines. One type prints out the contents of certain

memory locations after a program has stopped. We call this a post mortem routine.

A second type takes a given program and allows it to be obeyed order-by-order while printing out information about the course of the program. It is often called a sequence checking code.

A third type arranges for information to be printed out at specified points of a program. It is usually known as a check point or blocking order routine.

8.7   POST MORTEM ROUTINES.   Library Routines C3, C4, C5. These are printing routines and have been arranged so that they can be used with little or no preparation on the part of the programmer. They are read into the memory with bootstrap input routines and are located in storage locations at the end of the memory, the longest occupying locations from 986 to 1023 and using locations 0, 1, and 2, as temporary storage. The end of each of the post mortem tapes contains 100 two-decimal-digit numbers. These numbers are used to specify the locations from which printing will occur. Suppose, for example, that we wish to know the order pairs in memory locations 540 to 549. Then we read in Routine C5. When it stops we find the number 54 on the end of the tape and place it in the reader. When the START switch is moved, the order pairs in locations 540 to 549 will be printed and then the Illiac will stop. If we start again we will get the order pairs in locations 550 to 559. Codes C3 and C4 perform similar functions for decimal fractions and decimal integers.

The programmer should keep in mind the storage locations used by the post mortem routines so that he will be able to take full advantage of these important checking routines.

8.8 POST MORTEM VERSION OF THE DECIMAL ORDER INPUT. Library Routine C1. This is a very important checking routine and is usually the first one used after a program failure. It compares the contents of the memory with the contents of the input tape. Only discrepancies are printed out, enabling programmers to discover which orders of a program have become altered while the program was in the memory. This is an aid in making sure that orders which should have been modified have been modified correctly and that no order has become modified accidentally.

This routine is used in the following manner: The Post Mortem Version of the Decimal Order Input is read into the memory in the usual way with a bootstrap input routine. It occupies storage locations 962 to 1023. The program tape is then placed in the reader after its copy of the Decimal Order Input, so that the Decimal Order Input is not read into the Illiac. Then when the machine is started the program tape will be read and the words created from it compared with the corresponding ones in the memory. When a discrepancy is found it will be printed on a line giving, first, the location at which the discrepancy was found, second, the word read from the tape printed as an order pair and, third, the word found in the memory, again printed as an order pair. Thus a typical line of printing might be

8-9

345 L5 000 40 354 L5 546 40 354

indicating that the left-hand address of the order pair in location
345 had become modified, taking the value 546.

It should be pointed out that closed subroutines which have
been used will usually have their links printed. This gives an indication of the part of the program from which they were last called in.
Interludes cause a large amount of printing because the contents of
the interlude locations are changed twice in the course of input and
are printed out both times.

The Post Mortem Version of the Decimal Order Input causes
the memory to be changed to the original state as it is being executed,
so that if the program is started the original program will be performed again.

If desired, only selected parts of the tape need be compared with the contents of the memory. However, when doing this it
is necessary that all the preset parameters pertaining to that part
of the program be input and that the selected part of the program
begin with a directive.

All post mortem codes occupy locations at the end of the
memory and all of them use storage locations 0, 1, 2, as temporary
storage, so that it is desirable when coding not to use these storage
locations for constants or numbers which may need to be printed out.
It is worthwhile to note that if addresses which are to be changed
are initially read in with their final values then no printing will

take place on the post mortem if they have been modified correctly.

8.9   THE ADDRESS SEARCH ROUTINE.   Library Routine C2.
Programs sometimes fail because of a transfer of control to an order
which causes the machine to stop. The usual order causing the stop
is a zero left shift order because the memory is normally cleared to
zeros before a new program is read in.

Under such circumstances the offending transfer of control
order may be searched for with the aid of Library Routine C2. The
search routine is read into the memory, occupying storage locations
normally occupied by the Decimal Order Input. Next the address to
be searched for is read into the machine as a three character sexadecimal address. The routine then searches the memory (exclusive
of itself) for order pairs containing this address. When found they
are printed out (in sexadecimal form) together with their location
(in sexadecimal form).

The routine naturally has other similar uses. For example,
if it is known that some number becomes modified but it is not known
why, then the store order which does the damage can be sought for in
the above manner.

8.10   SEQUENCE CHECKING CODES.   Library Routines D2 and D3.
These routines control a program order by order and print out suitable
information about the execution of each order. This enables the action
of a program to be traced order by order. They use a blocking order
technique which enables a selected part of the program to be checked

in this manner. These codes are very slow on account of the printing involved and should not be used blindly.

Routine D3 prints out the function digits of the orders which are actually obeyed, starting a new line of printing whenever a control transfer order is obeyed. This enables the sequence of orders obeyed by a program to be traced.

Routine D2 prints in full each order that is obeyed, having one order pair per line of printing. After each store order or address order, the number transferred to the memory is also printed. This enables every step of a program to be completely checked. However, the amount of printing is such that this routine is very slow. It should be used only in the final stages of tracking down an elusive fault.

8.11 CONTROL TRANSFER CHECK. Library Routine D4. This routine takes charge of a program and allows it to be obeyed order by order. Each transfer of control that is obeyed is placed in a list kept in a specified place. The list is cyclic, that is to say, the later entries overwrite the earlier ones in a cyclic fashion. At the end of a program, the list can be printed, so that it can be discovered how the program reached its final end. There is no printing during the execution of the program, so that this routine allows the program to be obeyed at speeds much greater than those of the routines which print.

8.12 THE CHECK POINT ROUTINE. Library Routine D1. This

routine is designed to print out intermediate information about some other program. It uses the blocking order principle, and the programmer prepares a specification tape to describe the kinds of information he wishes to obtain. It is possible to go through iterative loops and print results on various passages through the loops. Data can be obtained as an order pair, a right-hand address, a left-hand address, a 10 character sexadecimal word, a signed integer, a signed 12 decimal place fraction or a signed 5 decimal place fraction.

Library Routine D1 is a very powerful checking routine because of the great latitude given the programmer in choosing where and how he will obtain information and because it utilizes the programmer's own knowledge of his code.

8.13   CONCLUSION.   The fact that it will be necessary to check a program should be kept in mind when writing it. Its storage locations, including those of the temporary storage, should not interfere with routines likely to be used in diagnosing its faults. The program tape should end with a stop control transfer to the decimal order input as explained in Section 8.4.

Occasionally a blunder turns up in the blind spot of the programmer and it appears to be impossible to find it. It is not much comfort to him to point out that the blunder can be found by continually narrowing down the section of the code in which it is known to be. This is tedious but eventually all blunders yield to this technique. A final word to this chapter might be that all programmers make mistakes but good programmers find theirs first.

8-13

CHAPTER 9

TAPE PREPARATION

9.1   THE ILLIAC INPUT.   The input unit of the Illiac
is a photoelectric tape reader that transfers binary digits from a
punched paper tape to the A register. The tape preparation equipment is used to translate instructions and data from the programmer's
manuscript into a binary-coded punched tape acceptable to the Illiac.

9.2   THE ILLIAC OUTPUT.   Output from the Illiac is
usually in the form of punched tape. This tape may be printed on
any of the Teletype page printers that are a part of the tape preparation equipment. The page printer performs a conversion from the
binary-coded representation on the tape to the sexadecimal or decimal
characters on the printed page.

9.3   THE PERFORATED TAPE.   SEXADECIMAL TAPE CODE CHARACTERS.
The tape preparation equipment presently in use consists of Teletype
equipment which has been modified to correspond to the Illiac tape
code. This tape code is shown in Figure 9.1. The paper tape can be
punched in any one of 6 positions across its width. One of these
positions is always punched. This is the feed hole or sprocket hole
position. Feed holes are smaller than the other holes.

Four of the remaining positions are used to represent the
2^4 sexadecimal characters. There are 16 keys on the Teletype tape
punch labeled 0 through 9 and K, S, N, J, F, L. When one of these

0 1 2 3 4 5 6 7 8 9 K S N J F L

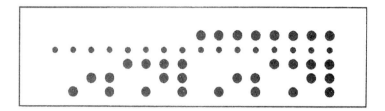

Figure 9.1

Sexadecimal Tape Codes

Delay   Space

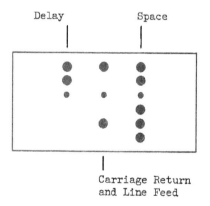

Carriage Return
and Line Feed

Figure 9.2

Format Tape Codes

keys is pressed a corresponding pattern of holes is punched across the width of the tape. Since a hole or absence of a hole is a binary affair, we speak of the character punched in the 4 positions across the tape as a binary tape code for the corresponding sexadecimal digit. If we speak of only the 10 sexadecimal characters 0 - 9 and their corresponding binary codes, we call the characters punched in a tape binary-coded decimals.

The Illiac tape code for sexadecimal characters is very easy to memorize since the hole positions across the tape simply correspond to powers of 2 from 2^0 to 2^3.

Page Printer Format Characters. Punched tapes are converted to a printed page by means of a page printer. Three additional tape codes shown in figure 9.2 are used to control the format of a printed page. These codes cause the printer to space, return the carriage and advance to the next line, and delay, i.e., perform one printing cycle without printing anything. The space function is similar to the space in an ordinary typewriter. The carriage-return and line feed must always occur together. If the carriage is to be returned from near the right-hand margin it should be followed by a delay code to allow enough time for the complete return to the left-hand margin. Otherwise the next sexadecimal character would operate the printer mechanism too soon, and print the character somewhere out in the middle of the line. If the carriage is within 25 characters of the left margin, a delay code need not be used after a carriage-return and line feed code.

Notice that these codes all have a hole in a position that is never punched for a sexadecimal. This is called the 5th hole position. When a punched tape is placed on the Illiac tape reader the circuits cause any character with a 5th hole punched to be skipped over, i.e., not read into the computer, when reading in the normal way. (However, a special input order will read such a character; see the order code.) This means that in the preparation of an instruction tape, these format codes can be interspersed with sexa-decimal order digits in any desired way. Then when an instruction tape is printed these tape codes will control the printer. The usual method in preparing instruction tapes is to follow each order pair with a carriage-return and line feed code. This produces a single column print of words.

Tape Codes for Letters. The printer will also print all the letters of the alphabet for identifying headings and the like. Tape codes are provided for these and are shown in the complete tape code list, figure 9.3. To accomodate all of these symbols, there are also numbers shift and letters shift tape codes, analogous to the shift-lock on an ordinary typewriter.

A list of instructions to be used with the Illiac and the Decimal Order Input (See Chapter 5) to produce any of the tape codes shown in figure 9.3 is given in Table 9.1.

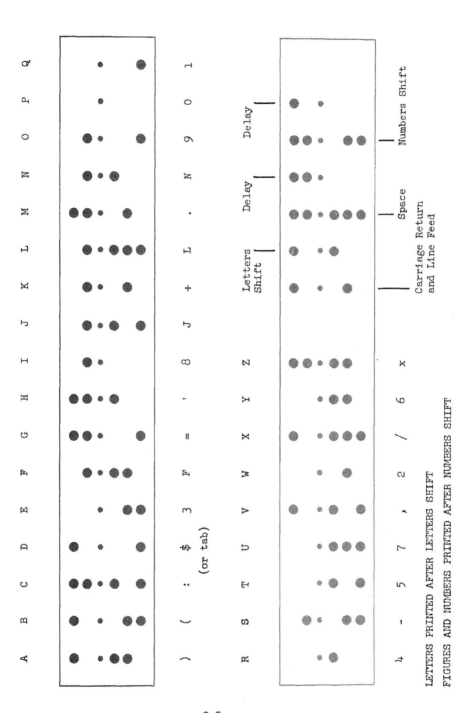

LETTERS PRINTED AFTER LETTERS SHIFT

FIGURES AND NUMBERS PRINTED AFTER NUMBERS SHIFT

9-5

PRINTED CHARACTERS	MACHINE ORDER (DECIMAL ADDRESS)
Space	92 963
Carriage Return and Line Feed	92 131
Delay	92 515
Letters Shift	92 259
Numbers Shift	92 707

AFTER LETTERS SHIFT	AFTER NUMBERS SHIFT	
A	)	92 387
B	(	92 195
C	:	92 835
D	$ or tab*	92 67
E	3	92 194
F	F	92 898
G	=	92 579
H	apostrophe	92 771
I	8	92 514
J	J	92 834
K	+	92 642
L	L	92 962
M	.	92 643
N	N	92 770
O	9	92 578
P	0	92 2
Q	1	92 66
R	4	92 258
S	-	92 706
T	5	92 322
U	7	92 450
V	,	92 323
W	2	92 130
X	/	92 451
Y	6	92 386
Z	x	92 899

Table 9.1

Coded Tape Operation of the Teletype Printer

*Only one printer has a tabulation mechanism.

9.4   <u>CLASSIFICATION OF OPERATIONS.</u>   The operations in preparing tapes may be listed as follows:

1.   Punching a tape from a manuscript by means of a keyboard tape punch.

2.   Punching a tape from one or more previously punched tapes. This operation is called reperforating and is used for duplicating tapes, joining short tapes, and making corrections.

3.   Printing a tape on a page printer.

4.   Comparing two tapes to see if they are identical.

5.   Comparing the manuscript with a printed copy (proof-reading).

It is necessary to punch the main part of the code from a manuscript by means of the keyboard. It is not necessary to punch routines that are in the routine library.

When all the parts of the code that have been punched from manuscript are correct, obtain any necessary routine tapes from the routine library. Using the reperforator, these tapes can be assembled into one long problem tape.

Every time a tape is reperforated it is wise to check the copy by comparing it with the original tape.

9.5   DESCRIPTION OF EQUIPMENT.   Several Teletype units are provided for making instruction tapes. These include a keyboard perforator unit, a page printer unit, a reperforator unit, a combination unit, and a tape comparer unit.

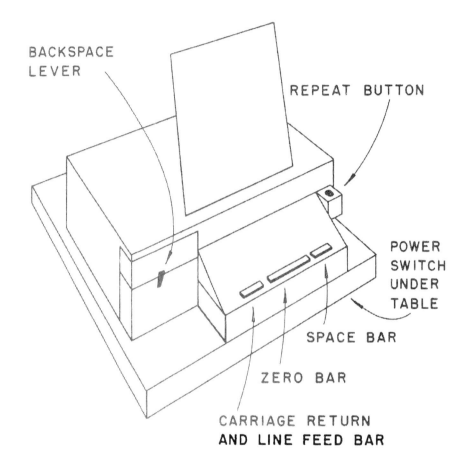

BACKSPACE
LEVER

REPEAT BUTTON

POWER
SWITCH
UNDER
TABLE

SPACE BAR

ZERO BAR

CARRIAGE RETURN
AND LINE FEED BAR

Figure   9.4

KEYBOARD PERFORATOR UNIT

Keyboard Perforator Unit. This unit is used to punch tape from a manuscript; see figure 9.4. Turn on the power switch under the table by pulling it forward. The power supply takes about a minute to warm up.

The sixteen sexadecimal keys that will be used most are in the center of the keyboard and arranged to be operated with one hand. It is recommended that a touch system be learned both for maximum accuracy and maximum speed.

If a wrong key is pressed, operate the backspace lever and then the space bar. This will punch the space symbol (all five holes) over the incorrect symbol and so be skipped on the Illiac reader if the usual 80 instructions are used.

Page Printer Unit. This unit is used to make a printed page corresponding to a punched tape; see figure 9.5. Turn on the power switch. The power supply takes about a minute to warm up.

In order to operate the printer mechanism the page printer motor switch should be turned on.

The function of the transmitter-distributor is to read paper tape and translate the binary tape codes into electrical signals. These signals are sent to the page printer. The binary tape code is sensed by 5 pins which are periodically pressed against the tape. A hinged lid holds the tape down against the pins. The tape is moved by a sprocket wheel which engages the feed holes punched in the tape. Place a tape in the reader and close the lid. Then turn the start-stop switch to start. The tape will now be transmitted to the page

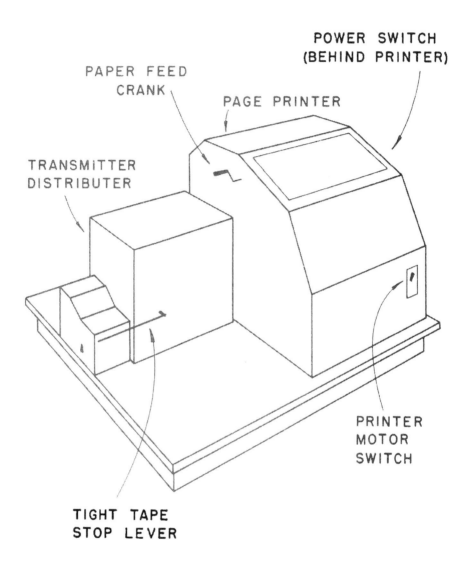

POWER SWITCH
(BEHIND PRINTER)

PAPER FEED
CRANK

PAGE PRINTER

TRANSMITTER
DISTRIBUTER

PRINTER
MOTOR
SWITCH

TIGHT TAPE
STOP LEVER

Figure 9.5

PAGE PRINTER UNIT

printer.

There is an end of tape stop device that stops the transmitter-distributor when the end of the tape passes under the lid. A tight tape stop bar will also stop the unit and keep the tape from being torn should the tape become snarled or tight and raise the bar.

Reperforator Unit. This unit is used to duplicate tapes; see figure 9.6.

Turn on the power switch by moving it towards the back of the table. After about a minute, the power supply will warm up and the reperforator motor switch should be turned on.

The transmitter-distributor has been described in the preceding paragraph. Place a tape in the reader and turn the start-stop switch to start. A copy of this tape will be made by the reperforator.

When a few corrections need to be inserted in a tape, punch a second tape containing only the corrections. Then use the reperforator unit to duplicate the correct portion; stop; insert the second tape in the reader and reperforate the correction; then replace the first tape and continue with the correct portion.

Combination Teletype Unit. This unit, shown in Figure 9.7, combines the functions of those units already described.

Underneath the top of the table are two switches. Switch 10 turns on the d-c supply which must be on before any of the other units will operate. On some of the tables it takes about a minute for the d-c supply to warm up.

Switch 9 turns on the motor of the transmitter-distributor.

9-11

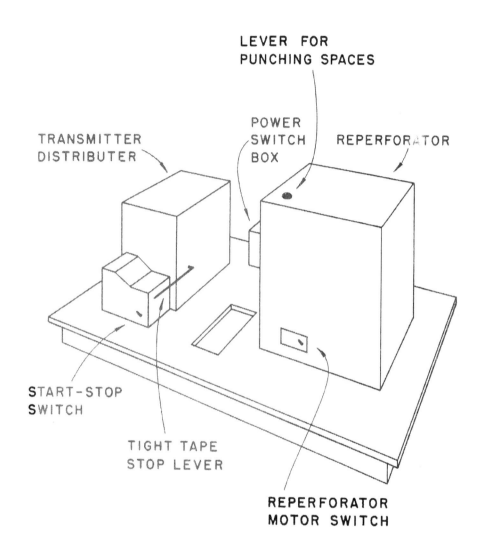

LEVER FOR
PUNCHING SPACES

TRANSMITTER
DISTRIBUTER

POWER
SWITCH
BOX

REPERFORATOR

START-STOP
SWITCH

TIGHT TAPE
STOP LEVER

REPERFORATOR
MOTOR SWITCH

Figure   9.6

REPERFORATOR UNIT

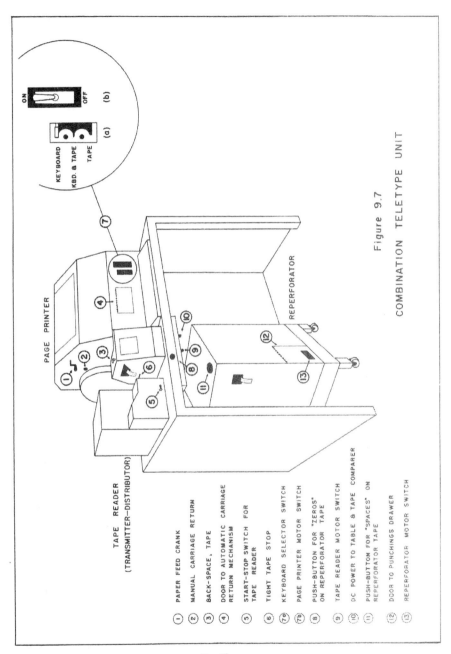

Figure 9.7

COMBINATION TELETYPE UNIT

① PAPER FEED CRANK

② MANUAL CARRIAGE RETURN

③ BACK-SPACE, TAPE

④ DOOR TO AUTOMATIC CARRIAGE RETURN MECHANISM

⑤ START-STOP SWITCH FOR TAPE READER

⑥ TIGHT TAPE STOP

⑦a KEYBOARD SELECTOR SWITCH

⑦b PAGE PRINTER MOTOR SWITCH

⑧ PUSH-BUTTON FOR "ZEROS" ON REPERFORATOR TAPE

⑨ TAPE READER MOTOR SWITCH

⑩ DC POWER TO TABLE & TAPE COMPARER

⑪ PUSH-BUTTON FOR "SPACES" ON REPERFORATOR TAPE

⑫ DOOR TO PUNCHINGS DRAWER

⑬ REPERFORATOR MOTOR SWITCH

The transmitter-distributor has already been described. It sends
signals to both the page printer and the reperforator and will operate
either or both of these units if the corresponding motor switch is on.

Turn on the reperforator motor by means of switch 13. The
reperforator will now duplicate any tape that is run through the
transmitter-distributor.

Pressing lever 11 will cause the reperforator to punch
space tape codes. Pressing button 8 will cause the reperforator to
punch zeros. However, one unpredictable character will be punched
at the end of the zeros. Zeros are useful at the beginning of tapes
to provide space for writing identifying information. They should be
followed by spaces to make it easy to set the tape in the Illiac
reader.

To operate the page printer turn on motor switch 7B. The
page printer will now print any tape that is run through the transmitter-distributor. The carriage may be returned manually by pressing
lever 2. Crank 1 will turn the platen.

It is possible to operate the page printer and the reperforator at the same time. However, it is possible for the reperforator
mechanism to make an error that would not appear on the printed
copy. If the printed copy that is to be proof-read against the
manuscript is prepared from the final tape, it is quite certain to
show any errors in the tape as well as any possible errors in the
printing mechanism.

Set switch 7A to "tape". Tape can now be perforated from the keyboard.

It is also possible to type on the keyboard, and perforate tape in the reperforator at the same time. To do this turn 7A to keyboard, 7B on, and 13 on. There is no way to back-space tape that comes from the reperforator. It is also more difficult to read the last character that has been punched on the tape than when the keyboard perforator is used for punching tape. The transmitter-distributor may be used to reperforate correct portions of a tape. The tape should be stopped before the error by means of switch 5. Type the corrections from the keyboard. Then move the tape to the next correct section and continue reperforating.

It is also possible to print with the page printer at the same time a tape is being punched from the keyboard. To do this turn on the printer motor by means of switch 7B and set switch 7A to "keyboard and tape". A disadvantage of this method is that the keys cannot now be operated as fast as when punching tape alone. There is no way to change errors on the printed copy that are corrected on the tape with the backspace lever. Since the printed copy is made by a separate mechanism at the same time that the tape is punched, there is also a small possibility that it may not correspond to the holes in the tape. This copy should not be used for proof-reading.

Switch 7B can be turned on and off without affecting anything being reperforated if switch 7A is placed in the "tape" position, before 7B is operated, and kept there while 7B is off.

Comparing Tapes. A tape comparer consists of two tape transmitters connected to checking circuitry. Place one tape in each reader and turn the power on. The tapes will advance in synchronism as long as the binary tape codes in the two tapes agree and halt if a disagreement is detected.

One of the present three tape comparing units will halt one row of holes beyond a disagreement. The others halt on the holes that disagree. The power should then be turned off and the tapes inspected visually. The tapes may then be marked if in error, replaced in the readers, and the unit restarted.

Two of the units have push-buttons for advancing either tape one step at a time while they are stopped on a disagreement.

Short tapes may be checked more rapidly visually by superimposing them and holding them up to a strong light.

9.6   GENERAL REMARKS. The misreading of even a single hole in a long tape can cause enormous changes in the behavior of Illiac. It is important to keep tapes clean. Dirt from tapes accumulates in the transmitter-distributor tape reading pins and causes errors. Worn or torn tapes will also cause errors.

Do not mark tapes with a waxed pencil: use a lead pencil or ink.

Library tapes and other tapes which need to be handled a lot are on a grey parchment stock which is heavier than normal tape stock. One of the reperforators is mechanically adjusted to punch this heavy stock.

It is generally more convenient to make corrections to be made on the tape itself, as well as on the printed copy.

If corrections are needed at the end of a long tape, it is sometimes more convenient to reperforate the tape tail-end first, so that the corrections can be made at the beginning, and then the reperforator left running unattended.

A hand punch is available and can often be used to change one or two characters and so avoid reperforating a long tape. Holes punched with it should be inspected carefully to see that they line up with the other holes in the tape. If in doubt, it is better to have the extra hole slightly oversized so that it is certain to be read by the Illiac reader.

CHAPTER 10

CALCULATION OF RUNNING TIME

Each programmer should estimate as well as he can the
length of time his program will run. This information is needed
for efficient scheduling of machine time and to enable the computer
operator to decide whether a program may have failed to stop when
it should have.

The estimation of running time consists of summing up the
times for executing all of the orders of the program, taking into
account that many orders are executed more than once. Thus, the
time is calculated for one passage through an iterated loop and then
multiplied by the number of trips through the loop. The number of
passages through a loop is not always known (as in the square root
code where the number of passages depends upon the quantity whose
square root is being calculated) and the programmer may have to
make rough estimates for such cases. He can make use of the code
checking periods to help him here.

10.1   ORDER TIMES.   The programmer must know how much
time the Illiac requires for each order. The order times are given
in Table 10.1, the time required for getting the order from the
memory being included.

The values given in Table 10.1 are in some cases not
exact. The 700 microsecond value for multiplication is a maximum,
the time depending upon the multiplier. It could be as low as 625

microseconds.

ORDER TYPE	TIME	
On, 1n	16 n	microseconds
2, 3, 4, 5, J	55	microseconds
3 not executed	18	microseconds
6	800	microseconds
7	700	microseconds
80, 81	4	milliseconds/character
82, 92	40	milliseconds/character in punch
	1	millisecond/character on display
K, S, F, L	75	microseconds

Table 10.1
Order Times

The time required to execute an 80 or 81 order so as to read one character from the tape is 4 milliseconds. Since most programs use conversion routines for input it will be found that the time is closer to 4 1/2 milliseconds for decimal input.

10.2 EXAMPLE OF RUNNING TIME CALCULATION. Let us consider a simple example. The program given in Table 10.2 will transfer the contents of memory locations 100 to 199 into memory locations 200 to 299. How long will it take?

The program in Table 10.2 consists of 7 words. There is a loop consisting of the 9 orders beginning with the left-hand order at location 0 and ending with the left-hand order at location 4.

This loop is executed 100 times. There are no other orders executed except the stop order. Thus we have the following orders:

```
      00 50K
0     L5 (100)F
      40 (200)F
1     L5 L
      L0 5L
2     32 4L
      L5 L
3     L4 6L
      40 L
4     26 L
      0F F
5     L5 199F
      40 299F
6     00 1F
      00 1F
      24 50N
```

Table 10.2

Repetitive Program

Five $\underline{L}$ orders at 75 microseconds,
Two $\underline{4}$ orders at 55 microseconds,
One $\underline{2}$ order at 55 microseconds,
One $\underline{3}$ order at 18 microseconds.

The time T is then given as

$$T = (5 \times 75 + 2 \times 55 + 55 + 18)\ 100 \text{ microseconds,}$$

$$= 53,800 \text{ microseconds,}$$

$$= .054 \text{ seconds.}$$

10.3   <u>A SIMPLE RUNNING TIME FORMULA.</u>   A rule which is accurate enough for most calculations is the following one:

Let N_0 = number of orders obeyed,

N_m = number of multiplication orders obeyed,

N_d = number of division orders obeyed,

N_s = number of shifts.

Then the running time T, exclusive of input and output orders, is

$$T = \frac{N_0}{16} + \frac{N_s}{60} + \frac{N_m + N_d}{2} \quad \text{milliseconds.}$$

In the example given above N_0 is 900 while $N_s = N_m = N_d = 0$. We thus have $T = 900/16$ milliseconds or about .056 seconds.

10-4

CHAPTER 11

PREPARATION OF A COMPLETE PROGRAM

The problems solved on the Illiac vary in complexity from
programs requiring only the punching of parameters and data for use
with a library routine to programs involving hundreds of words requiring the entire memory capacity of the machine. There is, of
course, no "typical" program; however, the problem described in the
following sections illustrates features common to many problems.

The problem described is one that arose in the electron
tube research laboratory of the University of Illinois.* The problem
is first described qualitatively, and a general mathematical formulation is given. Approximations are then made to simplify the
equations. The resultant equations are reformulated so that a
library routine can be used for the solution, and reformulated again
in terms of scaled variables so that machine range will not be ex-
ceeded. The general organization of the program is then described,
and the details of the coding are given. Those interested primarily
in the programming may omit the introductory description.

11.1 <u>GENERAL STATEMENT OF THE PROBLEM.</u> The purpose
of the problem is to solve for the trajectories of electrons in an

---

* The staff of the computer laboratory is indebted to Mr. Irving
Kaufman of the electron tube research laboratory for permission
to describe his problem and for his assistance in the preparation
of this chapter.

electron cyclotron. An electron cyclotron is a device that accelerates
electrons to energies of several million electron volts. The accelerating mechanism is a radio-frequency electric field in a microwave
cavity. According to the well-known Lorentz force equation, the force
on a charged particle is given by:

$$\overline{f} = q\overline{E} + q\overline{v} \times \overline{B}, \qquad (11.1)$$

Here

$\overline{f}$ = vector force (newtons),

q = charge (coulombs),

$\overline{E}$ = vector electric field (volts per meter),

$\overline{v}$ = vector velocity (meters per second),

$\overline{B}$ = vector magnetic flux density (webers per square meter).

It is seen that the component of force produced by the
electric field $\overline{E}$ is parallel to $\overline{E}$; that produced by the magnetic
field B is perpendicular to both $\overline{v}$ and $\overline{B}$. The former causes accelera-
tion or increase in energy; the latter merely changes the direction
of motion. This combination gives rise to the mechanism of the
electron cyclotron shown in figure 11.1.

Here a microwave cavity, externally supplied with electrical energy, is immersed in a uniform steady magnetic field (shown
by the dots) whose direction is perpendicular to the paper. The
cavity has been constructed so that near the axis it has a time-

varying electric field $\bar{E}$ that is almost entirely parallel to the axis X-X' and whose magnitude is given by $E = E_m \sin wt$. The magnitude of E_m is on the order of 5×10^7 volts per meter, so that it is possible for an electron passing through the 1 cm. gap of the microwave cavity to acquire an energy of 5×10^5 electron volts. (This corresponds roughly to the relativistic rest energy of the electron).

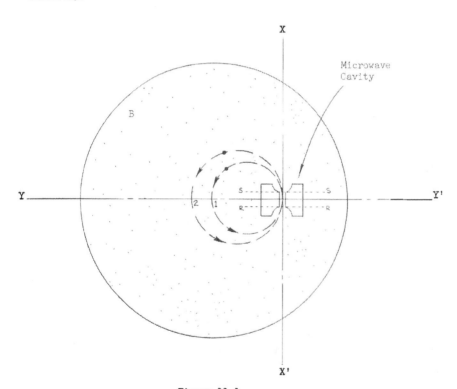

Figure 11.1
Electron Cyclotron

The action of this cyclotron is as follows:

1. The very high value of E forces some electrons out of the cavity wall during some parts of the cycle. (Let us consider here the trajectory of electrons emitted from surface R-R).

2. The E-field accelerates the electron toward surface S-S.

3. A fraction of the electrons emitted pass through the orifice in S-S. The magnetic field as well as space charge produces a slight bending of the trajectory.

4. The magnetic field external to the cavity causes the electron to move in circular orbits. The orbit radius is proportional to the product of electron speed and total (relativistic) energy. Consequently, a fraction of the electrons ejected are returned to the orifice in cavity surface R-R; the rest collide with the walls.

5. Those particles that re-enter the cavity when the field is in its accelerating phase (recall, $E = E_m \sin wt$) acquire additional kinetic energy during transit through the gap. They consequently execute larger orbits externally.

6. For those electrons that maintain the favorable phase conditions of (4) and (5), above, an indefinite number of orbits is possible. For a 1 cm. cavity gap, each orbit corresponds to a step in energy of approximately 1/2 million electron volts.

11.2 <u>TRAJECTORY EQUATIONS.</u>   The combination of the relativistic equation of motion for a particle and the Lorentz force equation yields, for electron motion in the cavity, the equation

$$\frac{d}{dt}\left[\frac{m_0(\bar{i}v_x + \bar{j}v_y)}{\left(1 - \frac{v_x^2 + v_y^2}{c^2}\right)^{1/2}}\right] = e\left[\bar{i}(E_m \sin wt - Bv_y) + \bar{j}\ (v_x B)\right] \qquad (11.2)$$

Here:

m_0 = rest mass of electron,

v_x = dx/dt = component of velocity in X-direction,

v_y = dy/dt = component of velocity in Y-direction,

c   = velocity of light,

$\bar{i}$ = unit vector in X-direction,

$\bar{j}$ = unit vector in Y-direction,

t   = time,

e   = magnitude of electronic charge,

E_m = peak electric field intensity,

w   = angular frequency of cavity field,

B   = magnetic flux density.

For motion exterior to the cavity, the term $E_m \sin wt$ should be deleted from equation 11.2. The two resulting vector equations are then to be solved for electron trajectories.

To reduce the complexity for a first order solution, three approximations are made:

1. The effect of the magnetic field inside the cavity is neglected.

2. The effect of v_y in the gap is neglected.

3. Particles exterior to the cavity are taken to move in circular arcs. The arc length is taken as the difference between a full circle and the cavity gap length. (In other words, the chord length of the gap is set equal to its arc length.) As before, the radius of the circle is proportional to the product of velocity and total energy. These approximations leave only one differential equation to be solved; for now, after some manipulations, in the gap

$$d\left[m_0 \, v \, (1 - \beta^2)^{-1/2} \right]/dt = e \, E_m \sin wt, \qquad (11.3)$$

while outside of the gap

$$\theta_{i,n+1} = K_1 \left[1 - K_2 \, (1 - \beta^2)^{1/2}/\beta \right] (1 - \beta^2)^{-1/2}$$

$$+ \, \theta_{e,n} - (2\pi) \, (n + 1). \qquad (11.4)$$

The symbols used in 11.3 and 11.4 and not previously mentioned are:

v = electron speed (meters per second),

β = v/c,

n = number of the orbit in which moved; i.e., for
first cavity crossing and exterior orbit $n = 1$, etc.

$\theta_{e,n}$ = the phase angle (radians) in the microwave RF cycle

11-6

at which the electron leaves the gap in orbit n.
(See Figure 11.2).

$\Theta_{i,n+1}$ =   the phase angle (radians) in the RF cycle at which
the electron re-enters the gap after completing
orbit n.   (See Figure 11.2).

    K_1 =   6.31599

    K_2 =   0.092910

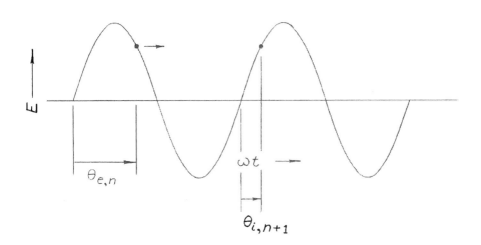

Figure 11.2
Phase Angles of an Electron

11.3

Electron Trajectory in the Gap. The equation of motion of the electron in the gap is given by equation 11.3, which is reduced to a set of first order ordinary differential equations so that the solution can be obtained using library routine F1.

Using as variables $\Theta = wt$, $u = v/w$, we can reduce equation 11.3 to the pair of first order equations:

$$dx/d\Theta = u,$$

$$du/d\Theta = (eE_m / m_0 w^2) \left[1 - (w^2 u^2)/c^2 \right]^{3/2} \sin \Theta.$$

The sine function may be evaluated by using two additional equations with appropriate initial conditions:

$$d(\sin \Theta)/d\Theta = \cos \Theta \cdot \text{ or } df/d\Theta = g$$

$$d(\cos \Theta)/d\Theta = -\sin \Theta \text{ or } dg/d\Theta = -f$$

The equation of motion of the electron in the gap has thus been reduced to the following set of four first order differential equations:

$$dx/d\Theta = u$$
$$du/d\Theta = (eE_m/m_0 w^2) \left[1 - (w^2 u^2/c^2) \right]^{3/2} f$$
$$df/d\Theta = g$$
$$dg/d\Theta = -f$$

Initial Conditions for Gap Trajectory Equations. An electron is introduced into the gap at $x = 0$ with negligible velocity $v = wu$ at a certain phase $\Theta_0 = wt$. The initial conditions are then, for arbitrary Θ_0,

$$x = 0, \ u = 0, \ f = \sin \Theta_0, \ g = \cos \Theta_0.$$

The effect of variation of the parameter Θ_0 will be studied.

Motion of the Electron Exterior to the Cavity. The electron is accelerated while in the gap and leaves the gap at $x = 1$ cm. with a velocity $wu_{e,n}$ and phase $\Theta_{e,n}$. It then follows a circular orbit at constant velocity and re-enters the gap at $x = 0$. The phase at the time of re-entry can be calculated by equation 11.4, in which β is equal to $wu_{e,n}/c$.

Re-entry Conditions for Gap Trajectory Equations. The re-entry conditions for the gap trajectory equations are:

$$x = 0, \ u = u_{e,n}, \ f = \sin \Theta_{i,n+1}, \ g = \cos \Theta_{i,n+1},$$

$$\Theta = \Theta_{i,n+1},$$

where $\Theta_{i,n+1}$ is calculated from $\Theta_{e,n}$ as indicated above.

Information to be Printed. For a given value of the initial phase Θ_0, the following information is desired for each of ten orbits:

(a) The orbit index n,

(b) The phase $\Theta_{e,n}$ of the electron leaving the gap,

(c) The phase $\Theta_{i,n+1}$ of the electron re-entering the gap,

(d) The relative velocity β of the electron in the orbit,

(e) The quantity $\left[1 - \beta^2 \right]^{-1/2}$,

(f) The energy of the electron in the orbit.

11-9

The calculation is to be repeated with different values of the para-meter Θ_0. The parameter Θ_0 is printed for identification of results.

11.4 SCALING OF THE QUANTITIES FOR ILLIAC SOLUTION.

Magnitude of Quantities Involved. For the range of in-tegration (electron trajectory in the gap), the phase angle Θ was known to be in the range $1 < \Theta < 2.5$ from a previous desk calculator solution. The design constants and physical constants are E_m, w, e, m_0, and c, which are, respectively, the peak eletric field in-tensity in the gap, the angular frequency of the field, the charge of the electron, the rest mass of the electron, and the velocity of light. The gap length of 1 cm. is the maximum value of the variable x. The maximum value of u is easily calculated, since wu/c is the velocity of the electron relative to the velocity of light and is less than one. The variables f, g, and their derivatives are the well-known and well-behaved sine and cosine functions. The maximum value of the derivative $du/d\Theta$ is simply the constant eE_m/m_0w^2.

The ranges of the unscaled variables and the values of the constants are indicated in Tables 11.1 and 11.2. The scaling of the variables is indicated in Table 11.3.

SYMBOL	DESCRIPTION	NUMERICAL VALUES		SOURCE
		Min.	Max.	
Θ	Phase	1 radian	2.5 radians	Previous desk calculator solution
x	Distance	0	0.01 meter	Design constant
u		0	0.017 meter/radian	w u < c
f	f = cos Θ	-1	1	
g	g = sin Θ	-1	1	
dx/dΘ	dx/dΘ = u	0	0.017 m/rad.	
du/dΘ		-0.029704	0.029704	$\dfrac{\sin \Theta}{(1 - \beta^2)^{3/2}} \leq 1$
df/dΘ	df/dΘ = - sin Θ	-1	1	
dg/dΘ	dg/dΘ = cos Θ	-1	1	

Table 11.1

Table of Variables and Derivatives

SYMBOL	DESCRIPTION	NUMERICAL VALUE	SOURCE
e/m_0	Ratio of charge to rest mass of an electron	1.7592×10^{11} coulombs/kg.	Physical constant
c	Velocity of light	2.99776×10^{8} m/sec.	Physical constant
E_m	Peak electric field intensity	5.2266×10^{7} volts/meter	Design constant
w	Angular frequency of the field	$(2\pi)(2.8)(10^9)$ rad/sec.	Design constant
x_{max}	Gap length	0.01 meter	Design constant
$\dfrac{e\,E_m}{m_0 w^2}$		0.029704	Derived constant
K_1		6.31599	
K_2		0.092910	

Table 11.2

Table of Constants (mks units)

SYMBOL	NUMERICAL VALUE		RELATION TO UNSCALED VARIABLE
	Min.	Max.	
ϕ	0.1	0.25	$\phi = 0.1\,\theta$
y	0	0.001	$y = 0.1\,x$
p	0	0.017	$p = u$
r	0	0.005	$r = 0.005\,f$
s	0	0.005	$s = 0.005\,g$
$dy/d\phi$	0	0.017	$dy/d\phi = dx/d\theta$
$dp/d\phi$	-0.29704	0.29704	$dp/d\phi = 10\,du/d\theta$
$ds/d\phi$	-0.05	0.05	$ds/d\phi = 0.05\,df/d\theta$
$dr/d\phi$	-0.05	0.05	$dr/d\phi = 0.05\,dg/d\theta$

Table 11.3

Table of Scaled Variables and Derivatives

The Scaled Equations.   The scaled equations become

$dy/d\phi = p$,

$dp/d\phi = E\left[1/2 - u^2/G\right]^{3/2}\ (2s/0.01)$,

$dr/d\phi = -10s$,

$ds/d\phi = 10r$.

The quantity in brackets in the equation for $dp/d\phi$ has

been scaled by 1/2. The constants G and E are:

$$G = 2c^2/w^2 = 0.00058078;$$

$$E = 20\sqrt{2}\ eE_m/m_0 w^2 = 0.84016.$$

The scaling for $dp/d\phi$ and for the bracketed expression have been absorbed by the constant E.

Scaling for External Orbit Recycling Equation. The time phase of an electron re-entering the gap is calculated as follows:

$$\Theta_{i,n+1} = K_1 \left[1 - K_2(1 - w^2 u^2/c^2)^{1/2}/(wu/c)\right] \left[1 - (wu/c)^2\right]^{-1/2}$$

$$+ \Theta_{e,n} - (n + 1)(2\pi),$$

where $K_1 = 6.31599$ and $K_2 = 0.092910$. Since $\phi = \Theta/10$ and n can be as great as 10,

$$\phi_{i,n+1} = (K_1/10)(1/0.1) \left\{\left[1 - K_2(1 - w^2 p^2/c^2)^{1/2}/(10wp/c)\right]\right.$$

$$\left.\left[1 - (wp/c)^2\right]^{-1/2} - 2\pi(n + 1)/100\right\} + \phi_{e,n}$$

where $\phi_{e,n}$ and p are values at the time of exit after the nth trajectory of the gap. After performing the indicated subtraction, the quantity within the brackets $\left\{\ \right\}$ is on the order of 0.01.

Additional Calculation for Printed Results. The additional calculations below are to be performed.

$$\beta = wu/c \quad \text{(relative velocity)}$$

11-14

$U_n/U_0 = 1/1 - \beta^2$ (ratio of total energy to rest energy)

$T = m_0 c^2 \left[(1 - \beta^2)^{-1/2} - 1 \right] = (511.24)(10^3) \left[U_n/U_0 - 1 \right]$

(electron kinetic energy)

After scaling we have

$\beta = wp/c,$

$0.01\, U_n/U_0 = \dfrac{0.01\sqrt{2}}{\left[1/2 - p^2/G \right]^{1/2}},$

$10^{-8}T = 0.51124 \left[0.01\, U_n/U_0 - 0.01 \right].$

11.5 CODING OF THE PROBLEM.

Organization of the Program.   The following steps are to be

done:

(1)   Read parameter ϕ_0 from tape and print.

(2)   Set initial conditions for integration in gap.

(3)   Perform one step of integration.

(4)   Test to see if last step has been performed; if not, repeat step 3.

(5)   Perform external orbit recycling calculation.

(6)   Calculate and print date desired for each orbit.

(7)   Test for last orbit; if not, return to step 2.

(8)   Stop, then return to step 1.

Use of Library Routines.   The following library routines

were used:

(1)	Decimal Order Input	X1
(2)	Constant Listing Auxiliary	X3
(3)	Differential Equations	F1
(4)	Sine-Cosine	T1
(5)	Decimal Number Input	N3
(6)	Print	P1
(7)	Square Root	R1

Use of Parameters. In order that the coding could be independent of the allocation of memory space, parameters in addition to those required by the differential equations F1 were assigned for memory locations of the subroutines. The assignment of parameters is as follows:

S3   location of first variable,

S4   location of scaled derivative of the first variables,

S5   location of first word of temporary storage for differential equations routine,

S6   number of differential equations to be solved,

S7   location of first word of auxiliary subroutine,

S8   temporary storage,

S9   square root subroutine R1,

SK   initial conditions setting program,

SS   main program,

SN   print routine P1,

SJ   decimal number input routine N3,

11-16

SF   sine-cosine routine Tl,

SL   differential equations routine Fl.

The parameters S3-S7 are those required for the differential
equations routine.

Use of Differential Equations Routine.   In using the
differential equations routine, a number of choices must be made,
as indicated in the specification sheets. These include:

(a)   selection of increment length h and the parameter
        m,

(b)   method for handling the independent variable ϕ.

It has been noted that two first order equations are required for
solution of the second order differential equation of motion of the
electron in the gap. Two additional equations were included to
evaluate the sine function required. The range of integration is
from $y = 0$ to $y = 0.001$ where y is one of the dependent variables.
Since it is not possible to predict the relationship between y and ϕ,
it is not possible to determine an increment h of ϕ in such a way
that integrating over an integral number of equal increments h will
result in y assuming its final value. The technique used is one
of integrating beyond the range desired, then integrating in the
opposite direction with a decreased value of h. The integration
then oscillates around the end of the range, with decreasing values
of h, until y lies within some predetermined interval containing its
final value 0.001. The initial length of increment h is determined

11-17

from considerations of accuracy and time. The value of h chosen was 0.001. For this value of h, the estimated number of steps of integration is 150 and the accuracy is on the order of 10^{-10}. The value of m selected is the largest possible such that none of the scaled derivatives exceeds range, namely m = 9, or $2^m h = 0.512$.

For homing on the final value y_e of the dependent variable y, the value of the scaling factor $2^m h$ is changed in the following manner.

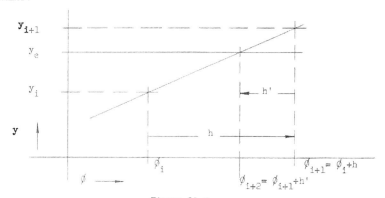

Figure 11.3
Adjustment of Interval Length

When $y_{i+1} - y_e$ differs in sign from $y_i - y_e$, $2^m h$ is changed to a new value

$$2^m h' = \frac{2^m h (y_{i+1} - y_e)}{y_i - y_{i+1}}$$

The integration then proceeds with the smaller interval h' (of opposite
sign from h) until two successive values of y again lie on opposite
sides of y_e. If, at any time, $\left| y_i - y_e \right| < 10^{-9}$, the integration is
complete.

In the differential equations of motion of the electron
in the gap, the independent variable ϕ does not appear. The value
of ϕ is calculated by using a counter in the main routine, rather than
integrating the equation $\phi' = 1$. The number of equations used is thus
4.

Details of the Coding.   The Initial Conditions Setting

__Program.__   Words 0 to 9L of this part of the code are devoted to
reading a value of the parameter ϕ_0 from tape (using the decimal number
input) and arranging the format and printing ϕ_0 in both degrees and
radians. (Print routine Pl is used for printing). Since the scaling
of ϕ_0 is by a power of 10, printing is arranged so that the decimal
point appears in the printed results to yield the correct values for
the unscaled quantity θ_0.

The remaining words are used for the following:

(1) Set initial value of orbit index n,

(2) Set initial values of p and y to zero,

(3) Set temporary storage locations for differential
     equations routine (S5 ff.) to zero,

(4) Calculate and set initial values of r and s.
     (The sine-cosine routine is used for the calculation),

(5) Set initial value of $2^m h$,

11-19

(6) Set initial value of $y_{i+1} - y_e$,

(7) Transfer to main program.

Details of the Coding. The Auxiliary Subroutine. The auxiliary subroutine is a closed routine whose function is the calculation of the scaled derivatives from the values of the variables in accordance with the equations of motion of the electron. The variables y, p, s, and r are in locations S3, 1S3, 2S3, and 3S3, respectively. The scaled derivatives $2^m h\, y'$, etc., are to be placed in locations S4 and 3S4. Constants necessary, such as G, E, and negative powers of ten, are obtained by using the constant listing auxiliary (Library Routine X3). Results of intermediate calculations are placed in temporary storage locations 1S8 through 14S8, for reference in checking the program for errors. The calculations are arranged so that none of the intermediate results exceeds capacity; otherwise the program itself is self-explanatory. The auxiliary subroutine uses the square root routine (entry from 6L), the first word of which is in location S9.

Details of the Coding. The Main Program. The main program can be subdivided into three parts; the supervisory program for integration in the gap, (words 0L to 18L), the external orbit recycling calculations (words 18L to 30L), and the orbit counting and printing routine (words 30L to 61L).

The first part of the main program performs the following functions:

11-20

(1) The independent variable ϕ is increased by h.

(2) Values for the ith step of the variables y, p, s, r and of $(y_i - y_e)$ are stored for future reference.

(3) The i+1 step of the integration is performed by entering the differential equations routine; i.e., new values of y, p, s, and r are calculated.

(4) $y_{i+1} - y_e$ is calculated and its sign is compared with the sign of $y_i - y_e$. If the signs differ, $2^m h$ is adjusted; if the signs agree, $2^m h$ is left unchanged.

(5) If $|y_{i+1} - y_e| \geq 10^{-9}$, another step of the integration is performed. If $|y_{i+1} - y_e| < 10^{-9}$, the external orbit recycling calculation is begun.

The second part of the main program performs the calculations indicated by the external orbit recycling equation in such a way that none of the intermediate results exceeds capacity. It should be noted that the quantity $\left[1 - p^2/G \right]^{1/2}$ is necessary for this calculation. To obtain this quantity, the auxiliary subroutine is entered directly from the main program. The auxiliary subroutine leaves the desired quantity in location 3S8, where it is then available for further calculation by the main program. It might be thought that the quantity could be obtained directly without re-entry from the main program; it should be noted, however, that the auxiliary routine was last used with intermediate values of the variables. For accurate results, it is therefore necessary to re-enter the auxiliary subroutine with the final values of y, p, s, and r in locations S3 through 3S3.

11-21

The last part of the main program, beginning with the right-hand order of word 30L, is devoted to orbit counting, and to calculations for the format of the printed results. The print routine P1 is entered in such a way that decimal points are placed to correspond to the unscaled values of the results. The format used is indicated in Table 11.4.

θ_0

degrees	radians
050.0000	0.872665

n	$\theta_{e,n}$ radians	degrees	$\theta_{1,n+1}$ radians	degrees	β	U_n/U_0	T
01.	2.07513	118.896	1.36207	078.041	0.863718	01.98428	00.503205
02.	2.00608	114.940	1.37242	078.634	0.942114	02.98271	01.013640
03.	1.98559	113.766	1.40726	080.630	0.967971	03.98364	01.525355
04.	2.00941	115.131	1.45802	083.538	0.979635	04.98157	02.035536
05.	2.05493	117.739	1.47955	084.772	0.985871	05.97197	02.541871
06.	2.07354	118.805	1.44881	083.011	0.989611	06.95861	03.046279
07.	2.04100	116.941	1.40483	080.491	0.992050	07.95137	03.553819
08.	1.99582	114.352	1.39111	079.705	0.993730	08.95100	04.064869
09.	1.98125	113.517	1.41901	081.303	0.994930	09.95242	04.576833
10.	2.00854	115.081	1.46613	084.003	0.995812	10.95028	05.086980

Table 11.4

Printed Results

LOCATION	ORDER	NOTES
ᵗ	00 3K	
3	00 F	
	00 320F	
4	00 F	
	00 324F	
5	00 F	
	00 328F	
6	00 F	
	00 4F	number of equations
7	00 F	
	00 200F	
8	00 F	
	00 340F	
9	00 F	
	00 64F	
K	00 F	
	00 220F	
S	00 F	
	00 250F	
N	00 F	
	00 125F	
J	00 F	
	00 74F	
F	00 F	
	00 95F	
L	00 F	
	00 153F	

Auxiliary Subroutine

00 200K

LOCATION	ORDER		NOTES
0	K5 F		
	42 18L		Set link
1	50 1S3	p	
	7J 1S8	$2^m h$	$2^m hy' = 2^m hp$
2	40 S4	$2^m hy'$	
	50 1S3	p	
3	75 1S3	p	
	66N 00F 005		
	8078 0000 J		G
4	S9 F		
	40 2S8		$1/2 - p^2/G$
5	32 5L		Waste
	50 5L		
6	26 S9		
	40 3S8		$\left[1/2 - p^2/G\right]^{1/2}$ at 3S8
7	50 2S8		
	7J 3S8		
8	40 4S8		$\left[1/2 - p^2/G\right]^{3/2}$ at 4S8
	50 4S8		
9	75 2S3		s
	66N 00F 00		
	100 0000 0000 J		0.01
10	7JN 40F 00 3401		
	6000 0000 J		E'
	40 F		
11	50 F		
	75 1S8		
12	00 1F		
	40 1S4		$2^m hp' = 2^m h (200S) E' \left[\quad\right]^{3/2}$
13	50 S8		
	L5 3S3		r

LOCATION	ORDER	NOTES
14	66N 00F 00 1000	0.1
	0000 0000 J	
	75 1S8	$2^m h$
15	40 2S4	$2^m hs' = 2^m h$ (10r)
	50 S8	
16	L1 2S3	
	66N 00F 00 1000	
	0000 0000 J	
17	75 1S8	
	40 3S4	$2^m hr' = 2^m h$ (-10S)
18	32 18L	Waste
	22 ( )L By 0'	

	00 220K	Set initial conditions
0	41 S8	
	92 149F	
1	92 513F	
	92 961F	
2	40 5S8	$\emptyset$
	50 2L	
3	26 SJ	$\longrightarrow$ D.N.I. Input $\emptyset$
	L5 5S8	Waste
4	52 73F	
	50 4L	
5	26 SN	$\longrightarrow$ Print routine. Print $\emptyset$ (degrees)
	L5 5S8	
6	50 S8	
	66N 40F 00 729	
	5779 5131 J	$1.8/\pi$

11-26

LOCATION	ORDER		NOTES
7	S5 F		
	40 5S8		
8	52 71F		
	50 8L		
9	26 SN		Print ϕ in radians
	92 129F		
10	92 513F		
	19 5F		Set n+1 = 2 x 2^{-7}
11	40 6S8		
	41 1S3		Set p to 0
12	41 S3		Set y to 0
	41 S5		
13	41 1S5		
	41 2S5		
14	41 3S5		
	L5 5S8		ϕ
15	50 S8		
	00 2F		
16	L4 5S8	5 ϕ in A	
	50 16L		
17	26 SF	⟶	Sine cosine routine
5	40 7S8		
18	7JN 00F 00 100		
	0000 0000 J		0.01
	40 2S3		s = 1/200 sin 10 ϕ
19	50 7S8		
	7JN 00F 00		
	100 0000 0000 J		0.01
20	40 3S3		r = 1/200 cos 10 ϕ
	L5N 00F 00 5120		
	0000 0000 J		$2^m h$

Set starting values

LOCATION	ORDER	NOTES
21	40 1S8	Set $2^m h$
	L1N 00F 00 10	
	0000 0000 J	0.001
22	40 8S8	Set $(y_0 - y_e)$
	26 SS	

MAIN ROUTINE

	00 250K	
0	L5 1S8	$2^m h$
	10 9F	h in A
1	L4 5S8	
	40 5S8	Replace $\emptyset$ by $\emptyset + h$
2	L5 S3	
	40 4S5	
3	L5 1S3	
	40 5S5	Store old values of y, p, s, r
4	L5 2S3	
	40 6S5	
5	L5 3S3	
	40 7S5	
6	L5 8S8	
	40 9S8	Store $(y_i - y_e)$
7	00 9F	
	50 7L	
8	26 SL	Differential equations Routine F1
	L5 S3	
9	LON 00F 00 10	
	0000 0000 J	$y_e = 0.001$
	40 8S8	

LOCATION	ORDER		NOTES
10	36 12L		
	L5 9S8		
11	36 13L		If $y_i - y_e$ and $y_{i+1} - y_e$ agree in
	26 17L		sign, integrate again
12	L5 9S8		
	36 17L		
13	L5 4S5	y_i	If $y_i - y_e$ and $y_{i+1} - y_e$ disagree
	L0 S3	y_{i+1}	in sign, form $2^m h'$
14	40 10S8	$y_i - y_{i+1}$	
	50 8S8	$(y_{i+1} - y_e)$	
15	75 1S8	$2^m h$	
	66 10S8		
16	S5 F		
	40 1S8		$2^m h' = 2^m h(y_{i+1} - y_e)/(y_i - y_{i+1})$
17	L7 8S8		
	L0N 00F 00		
	1000 J		Is $\lvert y_i - y_e \rvert < 10^{-9}$?
18	36 L		
	50 18L		
19	26 S7	⟶	Auxiliary subroutine
	L5N 00F 00 446		
	6080 0000 J		M
20	50 S8		
	66 3S8		
21	S5 F		
	40 11S8		
22	L1N 00F 00		
	10000 0000 J		10^{-3}
	50 S8		
23	66 1S3		
	S5 F		

LOCATION	ORDER	NOTES
24	40 12S8	$-10^{-3}/p$
	50 6S8 $(n+1)2^{-7}$	
25	7JN 00F 00 1000	
	0000 0000 J	0.1
	40 F	
26	50 F	
	75N 40F 00 1283	
	1800 0000 J	I
27	00 7F	
	10 11S8	
28	L0 12S8	
	66N 00F 00 1000	
	0000 0000 J	0.1
29	S1 F	
	L4 5S8	$\phi_{e,n}$
30	40 13S8	$\phi_{i,n+1}$
	92 129F	
31	92 513F	
	L5 6S8	
32	LON 01F 00F	$n \times 2^{-7}$
	10 32F	
33	J0 22F	
	50 33L	
34	26 SN	Print n
	L5 5S8	
35	52 61F	
	50 35L	
36	26 SN	Print $\phi_{e,n}$ in radians
	50N 40F 00 729	
	5779 5131 J	

LOCATION	ORDER	NOTES
37	7J 5S8	
	22 38L √	Waste
38	52 63F	Print $\phi_{e,n}$ in degrees
	50 38L	
39	26 SN	
	L5 13S8	
40	40 5S8	Set ϕ for next integration
	22 41L Waste	
41	52 61F	
	50 41L	
42	26 SN	Print $\phi_{i,n+1}$ in radians
	50N 40F 00729	
	5779 5131 J	$1.8/\pi$
43	7J 13S8	
	22 44L Waste	
44	52 63F	
	50 44L	
45	26 SN	Print $\phi_{i,n+1}$ in degrees
	36 46L Waste	
46	L5 1S3	
	50 S8	
47	66N 00F 00 170	
	4100 0000 J	Calculate and print
	7JN 00F 00 1000	
	0000 0000 J	
48	52 71F	
	50 48L	
49	26 SN	
	L5N 00F 00 70	
	7106 7812 J	

LOCATION	ORDER	NOTES
50	50 S8	
	66 3S8	
51	S5 F	Calculate and print
	40 14S8	$\left[1 - \beta^2\right]^{-1/2}$
52	52 72F	
	50 52L	
53	26 SN	
	L5 14S8	
54	LON 00F 00 100	
	0000 0000 J	
	40 F	Calculate and print energy (mev.)
55	50N 40F 00 112	
	4000 0000 J	
	7J F	
56	52 82F	
	50 56L	
57	26 SN	
	L5 6S8	
58	L4N 01F 00F	Increase n
	40 6S8	
59	LON ONF 00F	
	34 SK	If n=11 stop, read in new ϕ_0
60	26 12SK	If n < 11, integrate again
	00 F	

Temporary Storage Starting at Memory Location 340

0	0
1	$2^m h$

LOCATION	ORDER	NOTES
2		$1/2 - p^2/G$
3		$\left[1/2 - p^2/G \right]^{1/2}$
4		$\left[1/2 - p^2/G \right]^{3/2}$
5		ϕ
6		$(n+1)\, 2^{-7}$
7		$1/2 \cos 10\, \phi$
8		$(y_{i+1} - y_e)$
9		$(y_i - y_e)$
10		$y_i - y_{i+1}$
11		$M \left[1/2 - p^2/G \right]^{-1/2}$
12		$-10^{-3}/p$
13		ϕ_i
14		$\left[1 - \beta^2 \right]^{-1/2}$

Allocation of Memory Space. Memory space was allocated as follows:

3-15	parameters
16-63	available for list of constants for constant-listing auxiliary
64-73	square root routine R1
74-94	decimal number input routine N3
95-124	sine-cosine routine T1
125-152	print routine P1

11-33

153-193	differential equations routine F1
194-199	unused
200-218	auxiliary routine
219	unused
220-242	initial conditions setting program
243-249	unused
250-311	main program
320-323	variables for integration routine
324-327	derivatives for integration routine
328-331	temporary storage for integration routine
332-335	previous values of variables for integration routine
336-339	unused
340-354	temporary storage
355-940	unused
941-961	constant-listing auxiliary X3
962-998	available for post mortem D.O.I. (Library Routine C1)
999-1023	decimal order input X1
0-2	temporary storage

Tape Preparation. The tape was prepared in two steps. The non-standard parts of the program - namely the list of parameters, the auxiliary subroutine, the initial conditions setting program, and the main program ---- were punched, printed, and visually checked for errors. Using library routines, the tape was prepared as follows:

Decimal order input X1

00 941K

Constant listing auxiliary X3

00 3K

List of parameters

00 64K

Square root subroutine R1

00 74K

Decimal number input routine N3

00 95K

Sine-cosine routine T1

00 125K

Print routine P1

00 153K

Differential equations routine F1

00 200K

Auxiliary routine

00 220K

Initial conditions setting program

00 250K

Main program

24 999N

26 220N

11-35

K06N

K055N

K05N

The tape was then checked for reperforating errors, using a tape comparer. The directive 24 999N was placed on the tape so that a correction tape could be placed in the reader before the program was started. Initially, however, the stop of the 24 999N directive was by-passed, and control was transferred to the initial conditions setting program by the directive 26 220N. The quantitites K06N, K055N, and K05N at the end of the tape are values of the parameter ϕ_0 to be read from tape by the decimal number input.

11.6   CHECKING THE PROGRAM.   The electron cyclotron program was typical in that a number of blunders in coding were made. A description of the sequence of events in checking the program follows.

When the program was first read into the Illiac, the quantity

07680. 00000 00528 59832 06685 86693 4983

was punched continually. The temporary storage was printed (P.M. routine C3) indicating that ϕ_0 had been read from tape and stored . (at 5S8). ϕ_0 was to be initially expressed in degrees scaled by 100 and was later to be converted to radians scaled by 10. Since the conversion had not occurred, the difficulty was isolated to the region 3L-7L of the initial conditions setting program. A subsequent printing of the orders of the print routine (with P.M. routine C5) indicated an incorrect link and the difficulty was isolated to the print routine entry (word 4L) which was

52 73F 50 2L rather than 52 73F 50 4L.

When the program was read into Illiac again, noises indicative of integration were heard, and after an appropriate interval of time punching occurred. The results were, however, not entirely correct. Values of $\Theta_{e,1}$ and $\Theta_{i,2}$ were incorrect, although some small comfort was gained from the fact that Θ_0 and n were printed correctly. The behavior of the variables $\emptyset$, y, p, s and r for the first ten steps of integration were then observed by using check point routine D1 with a blocking order placed at location 256 (6L in the main routine) ahead of the entry to the Runge-Kutta routine. The initial values of $\emptyset$, y, p, s, and r were correct, exonerating for the moment the initial conditions setting program, but $\emptyset$ behaved peculiarly on successive steps. Rather than increasing uniformly by increments of 0.001, $\emptyset$ increased by 0.001, then by 0.0246, by 0.0006, and eventually decreased slightly. It was finally found that the location 5S8 used for storage of $\emptyset$ was also being used for temporary storage by the auxiliary routine. This blunder was cured by replacing the orders 40 5S8 50 5S8 in words 10 and 11L of the auxiliary routine by 40F 50F.

With a somewhat longer correction tape, the program was again checked on the Illiac. The results of the first integration and orbit cycle were correct, but the results for the second orbit were all incorrect with the exception of the orbit index n. The re-entry into the initial conditions resetting program was checked and it was found that p was incorrectly being reset to zero; i.e., the program was robbing the electron of all the velocity it had gained during its first orbit. The correction tape increased in length; word 61L of the main program became 26 12SK 00 F rather than 22 11SK 00 F. The orders for clearing q_1 and p were interchanged in words 11L and 14L of the initial conditions setting program.

After the following code check, the results for the first orbit were again incorrect. After mutterings of "something is wrong with the computer", it was discovered that a terminating symbol had been omitted on the correction tape. The correction process then converged and correct results were obtained.

11.7 CONCLUSION. The preparation of a problem for solution on a digital computer is by no means a completely objective process. No two programmers would prepare the same problem for solution in an identical way. Furthermore, a second coding of the problem by the same programmer would differ from the first preparation.

The personal preferences of the programmer affected the electron cyclotron program in a number of ways. Memory space other than locations 0, 1, and 2 was assigned for temporary storage; it was felt that such an arrangement might aid in code checking. The S terminating symbol was used for designation of the locations of first words of subroutines, so that the detailed coding could be completed before memory locations were assigned to the subroutines. Thus, the location of a subroutine affects only one of the S parameters rather than the addresses of a number of orders in the program.

Among the changes which might be made if the program were rewritten is a change in the handling of the variable θ. If θ were expressed in revolutions, the overflow properties of the computer would simplify the recycling computation.

CHAPTER 12

THE CATHODE RAY TUBE DISPLAY

12.1   GENERAL DESCRIPTION.   Results of certain types
of calculations may be most conveniently obtained from the computer
by use of the cathode ray tube display. Whenever results of a
calculation can be represented pictorially as a graph or diagram,
the cathode ray tube output from the computer provides a rapid
and elegant method for obtaining these results. If results would
otherwise be graphed manually the cathode ray tube saves the human
time required for this additional processing and also reduces the
machine time required to present the results to the user.

     Another use of the cathode ray tube is to provide inter-
mediate results in such a form that they may be analyzed subjectively
during the course of a program. In this way the programmer may
discover errors in his program at an early stage in the calculation.
He may also obtain immediate results which may be used to determine
the way the remainder of the program is to be run. Even if the
final results must be presented with greater accuracy than is
possible using a graphical display, some advantage may be obtained
by supplementing the digital results with a graph or diagram. The
cathode ray tube output is called into use by turning the output
switch on the input-output rack to the cathode ray tube position.
When the switch is in this position the cathode ray tube is the only

form of output available to the user. The display on the cathode
ray tube is limited to a 3" x 3" square area centered on the face
of the tube. Within this square area, chosen points may be brightened
on a 256 x 256 regular square raster. A finer raster is unnecessary
because of the limited resolution of the cathode ray tube. This
limited resolution makes the display of digital information such
as numbers or figures somewhat unhandy. It has been found that no
more than about 200 fully legible numbers or letters may be displayed in a single frame. In general the requirements of the format
will restrict it to somewhat less than this. This disadvantage,
however, is somewhat offset by the possibility of using characters
having any shape which the programmer desires and by the greater
speed of output. A subroutine has been written which will display
characters at the rate of about 45 per second which compares favor-
ably with the rate of 20 characters per second for the punch.

In order to retain a permanent record of displayed results it is necessary to photograph the face of the cathode ray
tube. Two cathode ray tubes are installed in the rack. They are
driven so they operate in parallel and hence display the same
results. One is used for visual observation and the other is
equipped with a semi-automatic camera to permit photographing the
display. The film advance mechanism and the shutter are controlled
by the program while insertion, removal, and development of film
must be done by hand.

12.2 ORDERS CONTROLLING THE CATHODE RAY TUBE DISPLAY.

Orders which would normally cause characters to be punched or printed
will affect the cathode ray tube when the output switch is in the
cathode ray tube position. The conventional output order to use for
cathode ray tube display is 82 16. When this order is executed
it will cause one spot to be brightened on the face of the cathode
ray tube. The position of the brightened spot depends upon the
contents of the 16 leftmost binary digits 2^0 - 2^{-15} of the accumulator. Let these digits be designated by the symbols a_0, a_1, . . . , a_{15}.
Assume an origin of coordinates in the lower left-hand corner of
the square raster and let d represent the length of one side of
the square raster (d = 3"). Then the coordinates of the brightened
spot will be:

$$y = d (a_0 2^{-1} + a_1 2^{-2} + . . . + a_7 2^{-8})$$
$$x = d (a_8 2^{-1} + a_9 2^{-2} + . . . + a_{15} 2^{-8})$$

These formulae say, in effect, that the ordinate is obtained from
the first eight binary digits of A, regarded as a number, and that
the abscissa is obtained in the same way from the second eight digits.

During the execution of the 82 16 order the AQ register
will suffer a left shift of 16 places. This output order takes 800
microseconds. A variation of this order permits a spot to be brightened
in only 400 microseconds. When an 82 8 order is executed the ordinate

is determined in the same manner as it is for an 82 16 order,

$$y = d(a_0\ 2^{-1} + a_1\ 2^{-2} + \ldots + a_7\ 2^{-8}),$$ but the abscissa will be

the same as that of the spot produced by the last 82 16 order which

was executed. In this way time may be saved when several points

having the same abscissa are displayed.

Letter output orders are used for operating the semi-

automatic camera. The following orders are used for this purpose:

92	769	Advance the film one frame and open the shutter. (These operations start at the same time.)
92	513	Advance the film one frame and close the shutter. (These operations start at the same time.)
92	1	Close the shutter
92	257	Open the shutter

No effect results from ordering the Illiac to open the shutter if

it is already open or to close it if it is already closed. After

using the camera it is conventional to leave the shutter closed

with an unexposed frame in place.

Exposure of a single frame of the film takes place during

the period of time that the spots that make up the picture are

brightened. Amount of exposure is therefore controlled by the in-

tensity setting of the cathode ray tube and not by the shutter which

is left open during the entire exposure. Exposure of a spot may

also be increased by multiple brightenings. If calculations are made

12-4

while the frame is being exposed the resulting photograph will in
no way be affected although the image on the visual cathode ray
tube may fade partially before the completion of the frame. Advancing the film one frame takes one second and the Illiac will
wait until this operation is completed before executing other output orders. If the orders following the film advance do not involve output, their execution will be begun after only 200 microseconds.

No output orders other than those mentioned are of practical
use in the operation of the cathode ray tube display. A 92 order
having an odd address will affect the camera mechanism, while any
other output order will brighten a spot.

12.3   PROGRAMMING FOR THE CATHODE RAY TUBE DISPLAY. As
with typewritten output, the cathode ray tube display is usually
programmed by means of subroutines. If digital results are desired
the number of orders concerned with output will be greater when the
cathode ray tube display is used than when the punch is used. Information needed to form a character (such as a letter or decimal
digit) may be stored in a single word in the memory, but the
mechanism required to decipher this information rapidly may take
as many as 35 words. Such a device is used in library program
C01. This program uses 63 words to display information similar
to that printed by library program C3 which has only 31 words.

Graphical display is also most conveniently accomplished
by means of subroutines. Program O1 is an example of a subroutine

12-5

which enables one to plot axes and points on the cathode ray tube.
Any method of graphical display will almost inevitably require
scaling of the coordinates of the points to be displayed. Since
it is desirable to utilize the full screen area of the cathode
ray tube, up scaling may be necessary in some cases instead of down
scaling. The full screen is regarded as having a range of 1 for
both coordinates when library routine 01 is used. The full range
of all variables in this case should be scaled so as to correspond
to 1. If more than one graph is to be displayed on a single frame,
however, it is sometimes better to avoid entering the point plotting
subroutines more than once. Consider the following example: The
points (x_1, y_1) and (x_1, y_2) are both to be displayed relative to
the origin. Let us assume that axes have already been displayed
by program 01. The quantities x_0 and y_0 have been supplied to
program 01 when the axes were plotted so as to locate the origin.
They represent the x and y coordinates respectively of the center
of the screen in the coordinate system used. Let the necessary
parameters be those given in Table 12.1:

LOCATION	PARAMETER	
10	x_0	Assume these coordinates have been
11	y_0	properly scaled before being stored.
12	x_1	
13	y_1	
14	y_2	
15	scaling factor for y_1	
16	scaling factor for y_2	
17	1/2	

Table 12.1

Parameters for Cathode Ray Tube Display

A program to plot the two points might be the one given in Table

12.2:

p	50 13	scale y_1
	7J 15	
p+1	JO 12	plot (x_1, y_1) by use of subroutine
	50 p+1 01	
p+2	26 (to program 01)	
	50 14	scale y_2
p+3	7J 16	
	L4 17	prepare $2(y_2 + 1/2 - y_0)$
p+4	LO 11	to be displayed
	00 1	
p+5	82 8	plot (x_1, y_2) without use of a subroutine

Table 12.2

Program for Cathode Ray Tube Display

In the program of Table 12.2 the second ordinate y_2 is first scaled and then translated so as to be present in the accumulator in the proper form for display purposes. It is then displayed by use of the 82 8 order, thus saving machine time and also saving the programmer the trouble of re-introducing the abscissa x_1.

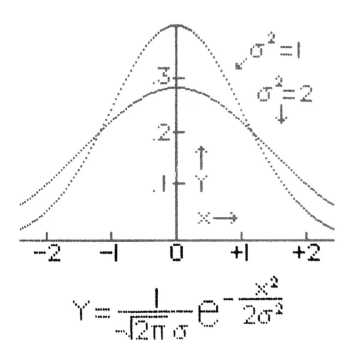

$$Y = \frac{1}{\sqrt{2\pi}\,\sigma} e^{-\frac{x^2}{2\sigma^2}}$$

CHAPTER 13

THE PROGRAM LIBRARY

The problem of planning and carrying out a large-scale computation is often almost entirely a matter of organization in which the detailed parts of the computation may be subcomputations which are common to many problems. Consequently, it is of great importance for the efficient use of a large-scale computer to have readily available to the programmer means for carry out these subcomputations. For example, it would be very wasteful if each programmer had to prepare his own routine for converting binary numbers in the machine to decimal numbers.

The program library is a collection of routines which have been prepared to make coding easier. They have all been machine tested and copies punched on tape are kept available for use. All are prepared for use with the Decimal Order Input (See Chapters 4 and 5).

The library programs may be divided into several categroies:

Input routines

Output routines

Functional routines

Problem-solving routines

Interpretive routines

Checking routines

13.1 INPUT ROUTINES. These are programs for transferring data on punched tape to the machine. There are routines in the library which will input decimals or fractions, singly or in sequences.

13.2 OUTPUT ROUTINES. These routines convert the binary numbers in the machine to decimal fractions or integers and punch the results as determined by wide choices in parameters.

13.3 FUNCTIONAL ROUTINES. These are routines which evaluate functions for specified values of the arguments. Included in the library are functional routines for finding the following quantities:

> square root,
>
> cube root,
>
> integral root,
>
> sine,
>
> cosine,
>
> arctangent,
>
> logarithm,
>
> exponential,
>
> legendre polynomial value.

13.4 PROBLEM-SOLVING ROUTINES. Problem-solving routines carry out more elaborate operations than functional routines. Those in the probram library include routines for carrying out the following operations.

Solving a set of first order differential equations

Integration

Solving a set of linear algebraic equations

Fitting a least squares line

Solving Laplace's equation

Minimizing a function of n variables

Interpolating

Inverse interpolating

Finding real roots of $f(x) = 0$

Multiplying matrices

Finding eigenvalues and eigenvectors

Solving Poisson's equation

13.5 <u>INTERPRETIVE</u> <u>ROUTINES.</u> These routines (see Section 4.6) carry out more elaborate "orders" in their own order code by using many Illiac orders. The library contains interpretive routines for the following operations:

Double precision arithmetic

Floating decimal arithmetic

Automatic coding

Minimizing Boolean polynomials

13.6 <u>CHECKING ROUTINES.</u> These are routines designed specifically to aid the programmer in obtaining information about his program. They are discussed in Chapter 8 .

CHAPTER 14

DEFINITION OF TERMS

A   2-5 *

The accumulator register or the contents of the accumulator register.

Access Time

The time to get a number from the memory to a register or the time to get a number from a register to the memory.

Accumulator   2-5

The register into which numbers can be put by addition; same as A register.

Action Cycle

The type of memory cycle in which the memory is connected to the arithmetic unit for the transfer of a number.

Addend   2-5

The number in the memory to be added to the accumulator.

Address   3-1

The right-hand ten binary digits of a twenty digit order; usually the location of a number in the memory.

Analog

Indicates a continous operation (as opposed to digital).

Arithmetic Unit   2-5

The part of the computer which is required to carry out arithmetic operations.

AQ   3-9

The double-length register including A and Q but excluding the first digit q_0 of the Q register.

*Numbers refer to pages.

Augend   2-5

   The number in the accumulator to which another number is
   to be added.

Binary Switch   7-4

   A portion of a program which is used to cause two separate
   sequences of orders to be followed alternately.

Bit   2-1

   One binary unit of information or one binary "digit".

Blocking Order   8-6

   A transfer order inserted in a program to stop the "normal"
   sequence of orders so that some check can be made on the program.

Blunder   8-1

   A mistake in programming, or more usually a mistake in programming which is most obvious even without running the problem.

Boolean

   Pertaining to the symbolic logic of George Boole, the
   mathematician.

Bootstrap Start   5-13

   A routine which, with only the aid of the original order pair
   80028 and 40000, makes it possible for the machine to continue
   inputing and storing under the control of orders brought into
   the machine from the tape.

Carriage Return   9-3

   The paper tape code which will cause the typing carriage of a
   printer to go to the left-hand margin of the paper.

Cathode Ray Tube Output   12-1

> The cathode ray tube unit which can be used to display results from the computer directly by output orders.

Check Point   8-6

> A point in a routine where some check is to be made.

Clear   2-4

> The operation of changing all the digits of a register to a common state, usually 0.

Code

> A group of more or less arbitrary symbols used to represent some other group of things.

Coding Error   8-1

> An error in the detailed preparation of a program.

Collate   3-27

> Digitwise logical product, same as extract.

Comparer   9-16

> A device for checking the identity of two tapes.

Complement   2-2

> See one's complement and two's complement.

Conditional Transfer   3-5

> An instruction which will cause a transfer from the pattern of taking orders sequentially if the sign digit of the accumulator is 0.

Control   1-4

> That part of the machine which serves to "control" the arithmetic unit, the memory and the input-output.

Control Counter   8-4

> Usually the order counter.

Control Transfer   3-5

An instruction which may cause a transfer from the sequential
pattern for handling orders; see unconditional control transfer
and conditional control transfer.

Counter

Usually a short routine which counts the number of iterations
carried out in some program.

-D-

Diagnostic Routine

A routine for finding and diagnosing a machine fault.

Digital   1-2

Pertaining to digits; discrete units.

Digitwise-complement   2-2

Same as one's complement; a binary number is the digitwise
complement of another binary number if and only if each digit
of the number disagrees with the corresponding digit of the
other number.

Directive   5-4

An order, usually on a tape, which specifies the location at
which a subroutine is to be stored.

D.O.I.   5-1

The decimal order input routine, Library Routine X1; used
as a general purpose input routine for almost all programs.

Double Precision

Pertaining to numbers of approximately two 40 binary digit
number lengths; hence requiring two registers or locations
for a single number.

Drum

A rotating cyclinder with a ferromagnetic coating used as a
memory.

Error

Mathematically the difference between the correct result and the computed result; often used in place of blunder.

Even Order   3-1

The left-hand order of an order pair, thus using digits 2^0 through 2^{-19}.

Extract Order   3-27

An operation which puts a 1 in the Q register wherever the number in the designated memory location and the number in Q are both 1, leaving all other digits zero; also called a logical multiply order because the resulting number in the Q register is the digitwise binary product of the Q register and the number in the memory; same as collate.

Fixed Address   5-2

The numerical address remains unaltered when put into the memory; usually in connection with D.O.I. where a fixed address is followed by an F.

Fixed Point   2-1

The binary point is always in the same position of a register; Illiac is a fixed point machine.

Floating Point

Pertaining to operations in which numbers are represented by a number multiplied by a power of a base; thus numbers may have different multiplying factors; floating point operations in the Illiac must be obtained by programming.

Fraction

A number with an absolute value less than 1.

Function Digits   3-2

 The first eight binary digits of an order; the T and V digits.

-H-

Hang up

 An unplanned stop of the machine due either to a machine
fault or a coding error.

-I-

Input Routine

 A routine for inputing other routines, usually aiding in
conversion from binary-decimal to binary.

Instruction   3-2

 The operation in the machine designated by the first eight
binary digits of an order.

Integer

 Pertaining to integers; although Illiac is a fixed point machine
with the binary point between the first two digits it is possible
to carry out operations using integer numbers less than $2^{+40} - 1$.

Interlude   5-11

 A routine which carries out operations and is then destroyed
by overwriting as the problem continues, usually carried out
during input of information.

Instruction Code   3-1

 The order code.

Interpretive Routine   4-9

 A routine in which a sequence of operations (instead of a
single operation) may be carried out on a number, the sequence
designated by parameters carried with the number.

14-6

Iteration

A sequence of orders, usually to be executed more than once, and arranged to converge to some analytic result.

-L-

Leapfrog   2-17

An engineering routine which may be used to test the machine.

Left-hand Order   3-1

The left-hand or even order of a pair of orders, thus using digits 2^0 through 2^{-19}.

Line Feed   9-3

The paper tape code which causes a Teletype to advance the paper one line; always in conjunction with carriage return.

Link   4-4

The part of the routine used to bring a subroutine into operation and designate the point of return.

Location   1-3

The designation of a number location, address or position in the memory.

Logical Product

When applied to numbers of more than one binary digit, the digitwise logical product; the same as collation of two numbers and the same as extract.

Loop   8-4

A sequence of orders which may be carried out more than once automatically.

-M-

Machine Error

An error caused by a fault in Illiac.

14-7

Memory   1-2

   A device which stores numbers; usually the cathode ray
   tube or Williams memory in Illiac.

-N-

Number Register   2-5

   The temporary location in which the addend, subtrahend,
   multiplicand and divisor are automatically placed by the
   control while the corresponding order is being executed; R^3.

-O-

Odd Order   3-1

   The right-hand order of an order pair consiting of the digits 2^{20}
   through 2^{-39}.

One's Complement   2-2

   Same as digitwise complement; each digit of a binary number
   is changed to get its binary complement.

Order

   A set of 20 binary or 5 sexadecimal digits which is used to
   define a machine operation.

Order Code   3-1

   A set of sexadecimal characters used to describe the operations
   in the Illiac.

Order Counter   8-4

   The counter which keeps a record of the location of the next
   order pair if no transfer of control is required.

Order Pair   3-2

   Two orders which are stored together in one location of the
   memory.

14-8

<u>Order Register</u>   3-4

    The register R_3 into which an order pair is transferred from
the memory just before either of the orders can be obeyed; R_3.

<u>Output</u>

    A display by oscilloscope, paper tape or Teletype printer of
the contents of some part of Illiac.

<u>Overflow Digits</u>   2-3

    The digits which, as a result of a computation, would require
digits to the left of 2^0 in a register.

-P-

<u>Page Printer</u>   9-9

    An automatic typewriter.

<u>Paper Tape</u>

    The common 11/16 inch width paper tape used for handling
numbers in and out of Illiac.

<u>Parameter</u>   4-7

    A number which may be altered from one computation to another
but is held fixed during a single run.

<u>Partial Substitution Order</u>   3-17

    An order which allows the address digits only to be stored
in the memory; a 42 or 46 order.

<u>Plant</u>   4-4

    The act of putting some number into an order or routine;
usually with reference to an address.

<u>Playback</u>

    The number coming from the magnetic drum memory.

Position

Referring to one of the 2^0 to 2^{-39} places of the memory or of a machine register.

Post Mortem   8-8

The checking of the routine in the memory after it has been used, usually by an automatic routine which compares the contents of the memory with the original input tape.

Program   1-4

The plan of a calculation.

Punch   9-1

A unit to punch holes in 11/16 inch paper tape, usually the punch providing output from Illiac.

-Q-

Q or Q Register   2-5

The register which must be used for the multiplier during a multiplication; also the register into which the quotient is placed during division; the contents of the Q register.

Quotient Register   2-5

Same as Q register.

Quadrature

The process of evaluating a definite integral by numerical means.

-R-

R_3 3-4

The order register; bottom row of 40 neon lights on Illiac.

Range

The set of numbers which may be handled in an Illiac register directly, from and including -1, up to and including $1 - 2^{-39}$.

14-10

Raster

The array on a memory tube.

Read-around

An index of the interference of one spot with another in the Williams memory.

Reader   9-1

The device to take data from a punched paper tape for insertion into Illiac.

Record

The process of storing a number on the magnetic drum.

Regeneration

The process of refreshing the stored information on a Williams tube.

Register   2-5

A row of 40 flip-flops which can hold a binary number.

Relative Address   5-2

An address which is relative to a directive and hence must be added to the directive address to get the true memory location.

Remainder   2-12

The quantity left from the dividend after a division process (without regard to Illiac).

Reperforator   9-11

A standard Teletype machine for making paper tapes from electrical signals.

Residue   2-13

The quantity in A after a division order has been obeyed (in the Illiac).

Right-hand Order   3-1

    The order using positions 2^{-20} through 2^{-39}; same as odd order.

Round-off   2-12, 13

    The process of adding 2^{-40} in multiplication and making $q_{39} = 1$ in division when the term is used with Illiac.

Routine   4-1

    A completed sequence of orders in coded form.

-S-

Scale   6-1

    The adjustment of a number to come within range of Illiac.

Sexadecimal   3-2

    A number system with base 16.

Shift

    The process of moving a number to the right or left in a register.

Sign Digit   2-2

    The first position in a register; 2^{0}.

Single Address Code

    A machine order code which has one address only with each order; Illiac has a single address code.

Slave Tube   8-4

    A device for displaying the entire contents of one memory cathode ray tube.

Store

    The memory, usually Williams memory.

Subroutine   4-1

    A routine arranged according to a standard pattern so that it can be easily used as part of other routines.

-T-

Tape Code   9-1

    The hole patterns in a paper tape that are used to represent numbers and instructions.

Tape Comparer   9-16

    A device to compare two paper tapes.

T Digit   3-16

    The first sexadecimal digit of an instruction.

Temporary Storage

    Locations in the memory used briefly during a calculation and not assigned to any number to be retained for results.

Terminating Symbol

    A symbol on the tape indicating the end of a section of code or tape.

Two's Complement   2-2

    The difference between 2 and the number whose two's complement is to be found; in the Illiac identical, because it is modulo 2, to reversing each digit and adding 2^{-39}.

-U-

Unconditional Transfer   3-5

    A transfer out of the ordinary sequential pattern of handling orders, regardless of the sign of A.

14-13

-V-

V Digit   3-6

>The second sexadecimal digit of an instruction.

-W-

Waste Order   4-3

>An order that serves no computational purpose but is
inserted because of ease in coding or limitation of the
machine because of odd and even pairing of orders.

Williams Tube

>A cathode ray tube used for storing binary digits.

Word

>Forty binary digits in a register or a single location
in the memory.

Working Space

>See temporary storage.

INDEX

-A-

y

CHAPTER 16

THE DRUM STORAGE UNIT

16.1   GENERAL DESCRIPTION. Auxiliary storage of 12,800
words is provided for the Illiac by the magnetic drum storage unit.
Some knowledge of the physical characteristics and mode of operation
of the drum storage unit is necessary for its most efficient use.

The magnetic drum is, physically, a rotating cylinder whose
surface is coated with magnetic material. Lengthwise, the cylinder
is subdivided into 200 tracks; associated with each track is a recording and reading head capable of recording digital information
on the magnetic surface and capable of reading data previously
recorded (Page 16-2). The periphery of the cylinder is subdivided
into 64 sectors; as a sector passes under one head, the digits of
one word are recorded or read. Thus, the selection of any one of the
12,800 words requires a spatial selection of a track and a temporal
selection of a sector; that is, access to one word requires selection
of one of 200 heads and the selection of one of 64 time intervals
during which the digits of the desired word pass under the selected
head.

16.2   COMMON DRUM INSTRUCTIONS. The record instruction
86 11 00p places the contents of A in drum location p and performs
eleven left shifts of AQ. The playback (or read) instruction
85 11 00p performs eleven left shifts of Q and places the contents of
drum location p in A. Either type of drum instruction must occupy a
complete 40 digit word.

Tracks
0 1 2 3 4

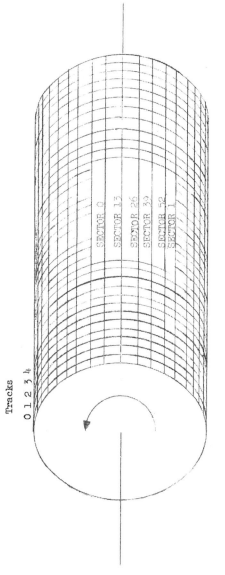

SECTOR 0
SECTOR 13
SECTOR 26
SECTOR 39
SECTOR 52
SECTOR 1

Figure 16.1

MAGNETIC DRUM

The address p of either drum instruction is specified by the rightmost 14 binary digits (2^{-26} to 2^{-39}) of the 40 digit instruction and hence is obeyed modulo 2^{14} = 16,384. It is restricted to the range $0 \leq p < 12,800$ for playback and $2560 \leq p < 12,800$ for record, with the interpretation in both cases being made modulo 2^{14}. Of the 14 binary digits specifying p, the least significant six (2^{-34} to 2^{-29}) determine in which of sixty-four sectors the desired word lies; the remaining eight (2^{-26} to 2^{-33}) specify the track. Except in special circumstances, the programmer need not be concerned with the breakdown of the address p into track and sector addresses, since the track switching is automatic and imposes no special timing restrictions on drum use.

The section of the drum $0 \leq p < 2560$ is used for storage of the drum bootstrap and commonly used routines; no recording by drum instructions is possible in this range. If either the record or playback instruction has an address in the range $12,800 \leq p < 16,384$ (mod. 16,384), the instruction will cause the computer to stop.

For most efficient use of the drum storage unit, the desired sector of the drum should be approaching the reading and recording head when a drum instruction is to be executed. Subroutines for transfer of blocks of words between the drum and electrostatic memories require time for execution of other Illiac instructions between successive drum accesses; to facilitate such use, sectors whose Illiac addresses differ by one are physically five sectors apart on the drum surface (Fig. 16.1).

The circuits for switching from one track to another are
so designed that all words on the same sector are equally accessible.
For this to be possible, a delay of one word time precedes any drum
consultation.

As an example, suppose that the digits of word 0 have been
read from drum track 0, sector 0. As the drum rotates (Fig. 16.1),
sectors 13, 26, and 39 pass under the reading heads. This interval
of three word times is available for calculation and for address
modification. The drum instruction requesting consultation of
sector 1 should be in the Illiac order register before sector 52 begins
to pass under the reading heads. The enforced delay of one word time
occurs as sector 52 passes under the head, whereupon the digits of any
word in sector 1 can be read into the Illiac accumulator as sector 1
passes under the heads.

16.3   CALCULATION OF ACCESS TIME.   The timing data necessary
for efficient use of the drum storage unit can be deduced from the
following facts:

1. The time required for one revolution of the drum is 16.9 milliseconds.

2. Since the digits of 64 words are stored serially around the periphery
    of each track, the time required for the digits of one word (one
    sector interval) to pass a reading or recording head is 0.264
    milliseconds.

3. The drum instruction must be in the Illiac order register at least
    one sector interval (0.264 milliseconds) before the digits of the

word can be transferred between the drum and the Illiac accumulator.
Thus, the minimum time required for execution of a drum instruction
is two sector intervals or 0.53 milliseconds.

4. Words corresponding to successive addresses in drum instructions
are spaced five sectors apart on the drum surface.

An isolated drum instruction with no definite timing relationship to other drum instructions may be regarded as occurring when the
drum is in a random position. In this case, the time taken by the drum
instruction will be equally likely to lie anywhere in the range between
the minimum of 0.53 milliseconds and the maximum of one revolution time
plus one sector interval or 17.43 milliseconds. The average time would
thus be 9.0 milliseconds.

A program does not usually have isolated drum instructions,
but instead it will contain a sequence of drum instructions separated
by other Illiac instructions. Under these circumstances, three timing
calculations are of importance.

1. The time t between the completion of one drum instruction and the
completion of the next drum instruction.

2. The time T required by all the Illiac instructions which come
between the two drum instructions.

3. The maximum time T_{max} available for execution of Illiac instructions
if the second drum instruction is to be obeyed as quickly as
possible after the first.

The commonest case is that in which successive drum instructions
have successive addresses. The time T_{max} is then equal to three sector

intervals or 0.79 milliseconds. If $T \leq T_{max}$, then the time t is equal to five sector intervals, or 1.32 milliseconds. If the time T required for execution of Illiac instructions exceeds T_{max}, at least one additional drum revolution will be required for each access, giving t = 18.2 milliseconds as the time between completion of drum instructions.

A general calculation of t and T_{max} for arbitrary addresses of two successively obeyed drum instructions can be made in the following way. If the address of one drum instruction is p_1, and that of the next is p_2, one first calculates $5(p_2 - p_1) - 2 - 3.8T$ and forms its residue modulo 64. (All times are in milliseconds.) Call this quantity R. In other words, R is formed by successively adding or subtracting 64 from the above expression so as to make R lie in the range $0 \leq R < 64$. The time t between completion of the two drum instructions is then given by the formula t = 0.53 + T + .264R. The time T_{max} is chosen as the shortest time T to make R = 0. Thus one obtains

$$T_{max} = .264 \left\{ \text{Residue of} \quad \left[5(p_2 - p_1) - 2 \right] \quad (\text{modulo } 64) \right\}$$

16.4 CALCULATION OF TIME OF EXECUTION OF ILLIAC INSTRUCTIONS.
If access time to the drum storage is to be minimized, it is important that accurate calculations be made of the time of execution of Illiac instructions obeyed between successive drum instructions. The most accurate way of performing this calculation is to determine the number of clock periods of the Illiac electrostatic storage unit. The clock periods required for instructions commonly used in drum transfer routines are given in Table 16.4.

Location	Order		
10	40 11	L	2 readout order pair
	L5 (n)	F	4 order type L

11	86 11	F	2 readout order pair
	00	F	0 order type 86

12			2 readout order pair
	F5 11	L	4 order type F
	40 11	L	2 order type 4

13			2 readout order pair
	F5 10	L	4 order type F
	42 10	L	2 order type 4

14			2 readout order pair
	FO 35	L	4 order type F
	32 10	L	2 control transfer
			32 Total

The time T required for the record loop is therefore 32 x 0.0187 = 0.598 milliseconds, which is less than the time of three sector intervals (0.792 milliseconds). Successive words will therefore be recorded at the rate of 1.32 milliseconds per word, after the first word has been recorded.

16.5 OTHER TYPES OF DRUM INSTRUCTIONS. A more general type of drum instruction may be written in the form 8 V_1 11 T V_2 p. If T is 0, 1, 8, or 9 the drum instruction will be obeyed as described in the first section. If T is any other digit type the right hand half of the instruction will be obeyed as a separate Illiac instruction after the drum instruction has been obeyed. In such a case the drum

address is interpreted modulo $8,192 = 2^{13}$ while the drum instruction
is being obeyed and for this reason no hangup is possible. The
rightmost binary digit of V_2 is uniquely determined by the drum address
p but V_2 is otherwise arbitrary.

Possible choices for V_1 include 5, 6, 7, J and L. The
playback instructions have V_1 equal to 5 or J and both produce the
same result. It is customary to take $V_1 = 5$ for playback. The
record instructions have V_1 equal to 6, 7, and L, and they record N(A),
zero, and 1/2 respectively as may be deduced from the characteristics
of the variant V_1.

If V_1 is taken equal to 4 a playback is executed but since A
is not cleared before carrying out the playback the result will also
depend on the initial contents of A. The result of this instruction is
to shift A and Q left eleven places but during the shift to insert
zeros into right hand eleven digits of A rather than digits from Q.
A digitwise inclusive or (logical sum) of this shifted quantity in A
is formed with the word taken from the drum.

A number of other instructions exist which affect the drum
but which also have little utility. They include the cases:

a. Drum instructions with the left hand address different from 11.

b. Drum instructions with the left hand type digit equal to 9
    rather than 8.

c. Drum instructions lying entirely within the right half of a
    word. (These instructions will produce the conventional effect
    only if the address equals eleven mod 64.)

Since applications of these types of instructions to actual programs are so limited we give no description of their properties here.

16.6   MODIFICATION OF ILLIAC. The initial instruction pair 8002840000 which has been used to start the tape bootstrap was rewired so that the instruction pair 8500S40000 is used instead. This change will have no effect in the operation of the computer except when a bootstrap start is used, and even then the computer will usually respond in the same way now as it did with the original instruction pair. The differences may be noted as follows:

1. No D.O.I. is now required on the front of your tape since if the D.O.I. is omitted it is taken from the drum automatically and placed in locations 3F7 to 3LL. The additional locations 3F5, 3F6, 000, and 001 are used in this process.

2. If a tape bootstrap such as that appearing on the D.O.I. tape is at the beginning of your tape, the computer will handle it in the same way as it has in the past except that locations 3L6 through 3LL will be used before the bootstrap is read.

3. If your program requires the reading of a jump instruction by means of a bootstrap start, it must be altered. A jump instruction written as 2406400000 must be replaced by 00K24100N, while if the instruction 263F700000 is to be read on a bootstrap start this instruction may be omitted entirely. In any such case, the locations 3F5, 3F6, 000, 001 will be used and the D.O.I. will be replaced in the Williams memory.

The program which provides the facilities described above consists of a set of routines which are stored on the drum. The initial instruction pair 8500S40000 plays back a drum bootstrap which occupies locations 000, 001, 400, 401 on the drum and 000, 001 in the high speed memory. It, in turn, plays back routine 1 from 3L6-3L9 on the drum to 3L6-3L9 in the high speed memory. Routine 1 plays back routine 2 from 3LK-3LL on the drum to 3LK-3LL in the high speed memory. Routine 2 records the contents of the high speed memory locations 002-01L at locations 31F2-31LL on the drum to preserve them and returns control to routine 1. Routine 1 plays back routines 3 and 4 from locations 002-013 on the drum to 002-013 in the high speed memory and jumps to routine 3. Routine 3 reads one sexadecimal character from the tape to determine which routine should be played back next and prepares routine 4 accordingly. If the character 0 is read from the tape, routine 4 will play back part of the D.O.I. and routine 5 and will jump to routine 5. Routine 5 replaces the words in 31F2-31LL in locations 002-01L in the high speed memory and then plays back the rest of the D.O.I. Entry is made to the D.O.I. in such a way that the reading of the initial function digit 0 of the directive is suppressed the first time. This is necessary since routine 3 has already read the initial 0. Routine 5 occupies locations 3F5, 3F6, 3L9-001. All except locations 3F5, 3F6, 000, and 001 are covered by the D.O.I.

If routine 3 reads the character 8 from the tape a tape bootstrap is indicated and routine 4 is prepared so that it plays back routine 6 into locations 3L8-3LL and jumps to routine 6. All words of routine 6 are contained in routine 5, but entry is made at a different point. Routine 6 replaces the words in 31F2-31LL in locations 002-01L and causes the next nine characters to be read from the tape and stored in 000 after faking the initial 8 which was already read. Routine 6 then jumps to 000 and the usual tape boot-strap sequence has been started.

Other initial characters have been assigned as follows:

(1) Leapfrog

(3) Flying Leapfrog

(F) Drum Post Mortem Routines

(L) Store Post Mortem Routines

16.7 USE OF THE DRUM. The drum will most commonly be used by means of library subroutines. When this is done no special knowledge of drum instructions is required, and all problems of reducing access time to the "minimum" of 1.32 milliseconds are handled automatically by the subroutine.

Y-1 is a typical subroutine for transferring information back and forth from the drum. It may be used to record a block of r words on successive locations of the drum starting at location q provided these words are present in successive locations in the Williams memory starting at location n. One must enter the subroutine by means of the instructions

```
            JO  n
  p
            50  p

  p+1       26  --
            00  q

  p+2       00  r
```

in order to cause the recording to occur. Control will be returned
to the right hand side of p+2 after the recording.

The same subroutine may be used to play back r words from
successive locations of the drum starting at location q provided these
words were previously recorded by the subroutine. They will be
stored in successive locations of the Williams memory starting at any
arbitrary location n. In order to perform this playback and store
operation one enters the subroutine by means of the instructions

```
            50  n
  p
            50  p

  p+1       26  --
            00  q

  p+2       00  r.
```

In addition to recording and playing back a block of words
in minimum time, this subroutine computes a sum check for the block
of words, which is stored on location q + r of the drum. Upon playback this sum check is recomputed and compared with the recorded sum
check. If any word has been recorded or played back incorrectly, the
two sum checks will not agree and the computer will stop on the
instruction FF010.

In some complex problems one may wish to play back words
which do not occupy successive locations on the drum, and if this is
the case library subroutines are not practicable. For example, it

may be desirable to record a matrix in such a way that either a
row or a column can be played back with minimum access time. If
the matrix has no more than 65 columns, one may achieve minimum
access for either rows or columns by recording the elements of each
row in successive locations but recording successive rows 65 locations
apart. Thus, we see that T_{max} (as described in 16.3) is 1.32 milliseconds
for both rows and columns and corresponds to the usual "minimum" access
time. If the number of columns N lies in the range $65 < N \leq 129$ one
must record the rows 129 locations apart, etc.

        If a technique of this sort is to be used with the drum, it is
up to the programmer to write his own record and playback loops with
due attention to access time and to sum checking.

www.ingramcontent.com/pod-product-compliance
Lightning Source LLC
LaVergne TN
LVHW011941060326
832903LV00045B/113

*   9 7 8 1 0 1 3 4 1 4 5 3 4   *